Talk with Us, Lord

Talk with us, Lord, thyself reveal,
While here o'er earth we rove;
Speak to our hearts, and let us feel
The kindling of thy love.

—Charles Wesley

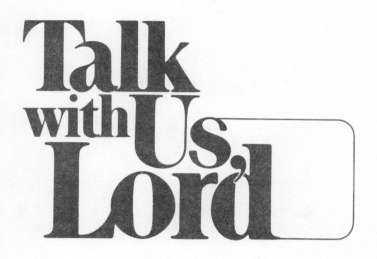

Talk with Us, Lord

Jayne Lind

Abingdon / Nashville

TALK WITH US, LORD

Library of Congress Cataloging in Publication Data

LIND, JAYNE
   Talk with us, Lord.
   1. Prayer. I. Title.
   BV215.L54   248'.3   78-12008

ISBN 0-687-41000-2

Old Testament quotations are from *The Living Bible,* copyright © 1971 Tyndale House
Publishers, Wheaton, Illinois. Used by permission.

All New Testament quotations, unless otherwise noted, are from The New Testament
in Modern English, © J. B. Phillips, 1958, 1959, 1960, 1972. Reprinted with
permission of Macmillan Publishing Co., Inc., and Collins Publishers.

MANUFACTURED BY THE PARTHENON PRESS AT
NASHVILLE, TENNESSEE, UNITED STATES OF AMERICA

To Jeff, Bob, Susan, and Tricia
—with prayers of love

Contents

Preface

It is very early in the morning. The sun is just rising, changing the mood of the landscape from stillness to bustling activity. The gray-green leaves of the olive trees glisten with dew from the night frost and the birds are awakening to sing their morning songs to the garden.

John, Peter, and James are sitting on the grass, talking in whispers. Jesus is kneeling a few feet away, praying. He has been praying for quite a long time. The disciples are talking about Jesus, discussing his prayer habits. He is so "religious" about it; every morning he gets up early and goes off by himself to pray. It is something he seems to need to do; it is as if the day won't go well if he doesn't pray first.

They have never known anyone who prays as he does. As Jews, they are accustomed to praying in the synagogue. They

9

frequently see Pharisees praying on street corners. But this is different. There is a quality about Jesus' praying which is unique, and they are curious about it. In a few moments, their leader gets up and walks over to them.

"Lord, teach us to pray," all three speak almost simultaneously.

Teach us to pray—to pray as you do, is the implication. And so the Lord did teach his disciples, that day and on many other occasions. His words about prayer are recorded in the New Testament, and, before that, the Old Testament also told about prayer.

It is my prayer that this book will teach you to pray. All the answers are not here, but the ones we were able to find through a study of the Bible are given, plus the personal experiences of many who have found answers to prayers.

Introduction

Father, I *pray* that this book will help others understand prayer and lead them into a deeper prayer life.

"I pray." What does that mean? Does it mean to ask? Or is it something much deeper than that? What is prayer? How does it work, or does it work? Is answered prayer just coincidence, the power of positive thinking? What role does the person who prays have in the results of that prayer, and is it more effective for two or three people to pray than for one person to pray alone?

The answers to these questions and many more about prayer have bothered sincere people for centuries—both believers and nonbelievers. I have been fascinated by prayer, amazed by it, perplexed by it, and as if it were the makings of an intricate watch, I have wanted to know just exactly how it works.

With this in mind, a small group of women began a Bible study for

11

the purpose of studying prayer, both scripturally and experientially. The following chapters are a summation of what we found.

We were not able in any way to pin prayer down. We came up with no list of pat rules and regulations which one can follow and presto! prayer will always work. But we did categorize prayer and systematically worked through our basic questions. Some definite rules were found. Some aspects of prayer that had puzzled us were very clearly answered in Scripture, and other misconceptions were seen to be unfounded.

And yet, when we were finished, we were forced to admit that prayer, like God, cannot be boxed up and neatly packaged. Just as he allows us freedom to act individually in different situations, so we must realize that he claims this freedom for himself as well.

This book may be used in two ways. It may be read simply for content or it may be used in a Bible-study situation. If it is used for Bible study, these suggestions should be followed.

All participants in the group should have some type of topical Bible. This is different from a concordance in that it lists Scripture verses by topic rather than by word. Without one, it would be difficult to do a thorough study.

Each chapter deals with a category of prayer. Before reading a chapter, look up all the Scripture references given in the topical Bible for that week's category. Keep a notebook and write a short paraphrase of the verses to help you remember them. Record your impressions, mark the verses which were most meaningful to you, and write out a summary of what you have found.

Proceed with the chapter after you have completed these steps. If you read the chapter first, the joy of discovery will have been taken away. Letting the Holy Spirit teach you directly from the Bible is so much more exciting than being spoon-fed by someone else.

When you come together as a group, discuss the chapter, and share what you found through your reading of the Bible.

Talk with Us, Lord

Chapter I

What Is Prayer?

An obstetrician is struggling with a difficult birth. The delivery is breech, which means that the baby has turned around inside the mother's womb so that the baby's legs present themselves first. One of the baby's arms is locked over its head, preventing the head from emerging. One, two, three minutes have passed. The baby's head must be freed, or the lack of oxygen will cause brain damage. The doctor has tried everything he knows, but the stubborn arm will not disengage. Desperately he whispers, "Lord, help me!" The baby's arm immediately slips out and the head appears—the baby gives a healthy cry.

A theologian in the sixteenth century rises early in the morning, kneels on the cold stone floor of his bedroom, and spends the next three hours in prayer. This, in his own words, is a necessity if he is to get anything done that day. The theologian's name—Martin Luther.

TALK WITH US, LORD

The Sunday morning service is drawing to a close. The last strains of the organ music fade as the minister says, "Let us pray." With heads bowed, the congregation listens as the minister prays for them.

Here are three instances of prayer, each quite different from the others and yet all are called "prayer." What is prayer? What is this mysterious exercise which, in varying degrees, is a vital part of every Christian's life?

Prayer means many things to many people; it is an umbrella word which encompasses multiple definitions. Yet in its most basic terms, prayer is communication with God. No matter what words are used or in what manner they are said, all prayer is at least an attempt to reach God.

Teresa of Avila taught that prayer is the raising of the heart and mind to God while being aware of God's exquisite love.

David, in Psalm 57, put it this way: "I will cry to the God of heaven who does such wonders for me."

The writer of the Letter to the Hebrews calls prayer "approaching the throne of grace" and goes on to say we should do so with fullest confidence (Heb. 4:16).

The definition which I like most is from David A. Hubbard, president of Fuller Theological Seminary, who says in *The Problem with Prayer Is . . .* , that prayer is our Declaration of Dependence. It is our admission that we need God; it is surrendering our right to run our own lives.

All these definitions are meaningful; they are the ideal, but in reality, is that how we think of prayer? Don't we often prostitute prayer? Is going to God with a "shopping list" necessarily being dependent upon him? We often get up from our prayer and go our own way, making decisions and striving after our own goals in total dependence upon ourselves, rather than upon God. It is as if the prayer were offered only as an insurance policy. "Wait and see if I can handle it, Lord, and if I can't, then you step in . . ."

One of the most startling facts I discovered when I first became a

Christian was that the term "God helps those who help themselves" cannot be found anywhere in the Bible. Actually it was Ben Franklin who popularized the saying, but it was Aesop of fable fame who coined it. The whole of Scripture repeats over and over again that we can do nothing without God. Even Jesus said that without the Father, he could do nothing. If we can do nothing without God, and if the way we speak to God is through prayer, then certainly we had better pray!

I feel that in order to understand prayer, we must turn totally around in our thinking. We are so accustomed to thinking of the word "prayer" synonymously with the word "ask" that it keeps us from the full knowledge of what prayer is meant to be. Asking is an important factor in prayer, and the Lord wants us to ask him for all sorts of things—ranging from new clothes (if we need them), to guidance. But there is so much more to prayer than just asking. If all we do in prayer is ask, then all we remember about a prayer is whether it was granted.

What if you spoke to your real father only once a day, or in some cases, once a week? And what if your conversation went something like this: "Father, I want to ask you for the following things"—then one, two, three, you read off your shopping list. What if, after a few cursory thank-you's and a quick affirmation of your great "love" for him, you went on your way, out of his presence until the next time?

Would your father be hurt? Would he turn his back on you and refuse the things you asked? No, being a loving father, he would probably grant some of the requests. But there was no communication, no two-way dialogue. It was a completely self-centered, one-way monologue.

It never occurs to us that God might have something to say also. We don't expect an answer except through the granting of our requests, so we don't stick around long enough for him to get a word in edgewise. If we think of prayer as conversing, rather than asking, it would help us toward a more balanced dialogue. We would tend to ask less, and speak more as we would in a conversation.

We have all had the experience of answering the telephone and

17

having the caller begin a long, boring account of everything he has been doing or tell us his problems. He hardly notices we are on the other end of the line. Soon we lose interest and are only half listening as he goes on and on, ad nauseum.

I am not implying that God does not listen to us, but I sometimes wonder if he doesn't feel like laying down the phone to go get a sandwich, knowing that when he returns we will never have missed him!

So one important thing to remember about prayer is that it is a dialogue, not a monologue. This does not mean God will always answer right then, and it does not mean we must wait for him to answer before we go on to say something else. It simply means we should give him equal time.

One of the misconceptions we have about prayer is that the desire to pray comes from us—we take the credit. But actually that is not what happens. God is calling us to come to prayer; we are not calling God to come to us. Prayer is an obedient response to the Holy Spirit's prompting.

The debate is not within ourselves. It isn't Self One and Self Two (our subconscious) having an argument which goes like this: "I don't have time to pray right now"—"Oh, yes you have—go do it." The debate is rather between ourselves and the Holy Spirit. When we kneel in prayer, the Holy Spirit has won the argument. C. S. Lewis says in *Letters to Malcolm: Chiefly on Prayer,* that when he calls upon God, God often replies, "But you have been evading me for hours." Maybe when we think of it in this light, we will be a little more willing to obey!

Categorizing prayer for study purposes is essential. Various chapters of this book describe different types of prayer, different reasons for prayer. Like everything else, prayer suffers under generalization. Each type of prayer must be understood on its own merit and treated as an individual entity—not all pushed under the umbrella word "prayer."

As we go through the various categories of prayer, no promise about prayer should be plucked out of context of the entire Bible. All

Scripture must be taken together, as a whole, in order to arrive at the full truth. Prayers for other people are especially complex because their wills are involved. Prayers for ourselves also involve our wills and we must reexamine ourselves each time we pray. God is always the same; his ways are always the same; it is we who are the variable factor in prayer. We change from one moment to the next.

The question which has fascinated me for years concerns the mechanics of prayer. How does it work? Why are some prayers answered immediately and others not at all? Is prayer just a mystical illusion which pacifies us in some psychological manner? Or is it a very real phenomenon, as certain as the ground under our feet and the air we breathe?

For a long time I had thought of prayer as some type of energy, as real as any of the physical energies present all around us. So it was with genuine delight that I first read Agnes Sanford's book, *The Healing Light,* and learned that she had discovered this truth long ago.

She describes the power of prayer as being much like that of electricity. It is a fact; it exists; but we have to plug into it. It is useless unless we use it. Until electricity was discovered, it was not beneficial to us here on Planet Earth. Only when Benjamin Franklin proved this power could be harnessed, and Thomas Edison made electricity practical, was it available to everyone. But it was always there. So it is with prayer. The power is always there—we only have to tap into it. Prayer is the means by which God's power is released.

Using another analogy, think of prayer as a radio wave. A voice is transmitted over a microphone through electromagnetic channels and then is sent from tower to tower across the country. Depending upon the number of watts a radio station has, the voice may extend from New York City to Los Angeles, or maybe only from Albuquerque to Tucson. If there is no obstruction, if no mountain range is higher than the transmitting tower, if there is no interference between us and the power of the radio waves, the voice will get through to us—we will hear it.

Now picture hate, envy, jealousy, and unforgiveness as obstructions. These are actually power blockages which keep prayers from getting through. The voice is spoken into the microphone, but it never goes anywhere because it meets an obstruction. The "program" is never heard; it is rendered useless. This analogy has been helpful to me in understanding exactly how prayer works.

In her book *Beyond Our Selves*, Catherine Marshall states that when we do not forgive others, God cannot forgive us, because we have shut the door.

This puzzled me. I knew it was a scriptural principle, but since God is able to do anything, I did not understand how he could be so dogmatic and rigid. And yet, I knew it to be a fact. I knew from experience that if I held a grudge against someone it was useless for me to pray for that person. The love was not there; I was praying from a cold heart and I might as well not have prayed at all.

In the eleventh chapter of his Gospel, Mark relates the incident when Jesus walked out from Jerusalem early one morning, teaching his disciples on the way. He had just told them that if they had faith they could move mountains. He promised them that whenever they wanted something, they had only to believe they would receive it and they would have it. But then he immediately qualified the promise, and we so often overlook this condition. Jesus said, "And whenever you stand praying, you must forgive any grudge that you are holding against anyone else, and your Heavenly Father will forgive you your sins" (Mark 11:25, 26).

Forgiveness is like a gate which must be deliberately opened before the passage of your prayer continues. A spirit of unforgiveness is a barrier just as surely as a wooden gate across a road.

There is a lot of talk these days about one's "aura." Studies have been made and documentation done by photography which seem to lead to the conclusion that all living matter has an aura of energy which can be seen; at least it can be seen with sophisticated camera equipment.

In other words, the energy which we expend anytime we move or speak does not all remain inside our bodies. When we run, we use energy much the same way a car uses fuel. When we eat, our body stores up fat and it is this "fuel" from which we take the strength to accomplish our daily tasks.

Speaking is also an expenditure of energy. The sounds actually come out and float on the air toward the person to whom we are speaking. It takes quite a bit more energy to shout than it does to whisper. The next time you are angry and shout at someone, notice how exhausted you feel afterward.

Have you ever gone to an exciting football game and yelled during the better part of two hours? You come away feeling emotionally drained. Part of the reason for that feeling is emotion; you really did want that team to win. But the other part is physical—you have used up a lot of energy by shouting.

Energy can also be consumed nonverbally. I went to a junior varsity basketball game recently. The crowd is always sparse—just parents and a few others who come to support the team.

The father of one of the players is very vocal about the quality of the referee's intelligence. He becomes loud and often makes a spectacle of himself. At this particular game he had a friend with him who was unbelievable. Together, they were creating such a scene that not only was I embarrassed for our school, but very irritated, as well.

So I turned around and glared at those two men every time they shouted at the referee. They noticed me but it didn't seem to inhibit them at all. I never said a word; I simply sat there and fumed, burning inside, and working myself up to a glowing (self-righteous) anger. When the game was over, I was exhausted. I had used up so much energy with my negative thoughts, and I was so tense, it took several hours to simmer down (literally to cool off).

This was an example of negative energy being expelled into the atmosphere toward others. The opposite is positive energy. How much better it would have been to pray for those men, to silently ask the Holy Spirit to calm them, to produce a miracle of change in them. Instead, I reacted negatively—my looks were just as destructive as words would have been.

21

Applying this theory to prayer, whenever we pray, either verbally or silently, we are expending energy. Our inner emotion dictates whether that energy will be positive or negative.

If I genuinely care about the petition I am presenting for someone—if my emotion toward the person for whom I am praying is love—then my prayer will find the right "wavelength" to be transmitted to God. But if I have negative feelings about that person, or if I am doubtful, or full of fear, I give off a negative charge (whether I am aware of it or not) and the prayer simply bounces around, never linking up to the Almighty Power Company.

At this point, let me state that I am not implying that prayer is a non-personal scientific formula and God a giant computer in the sky, receiving and relaying messages. The Scriptures record a very personal God who hears, and sees, and cares about us.

But this same God is the One who created all matter. And everything in the universe consists of matter. He set certain laws of physics into operation and we here on Planet Earth must live by those laws. Whether or not we agree with them or fully understand them, we still are forced to accept them.

When the woman who had suffered from an issue of blood for twelve years touched the hem of Jesus' garment and was healed, Jesus asked who touched him, for he "knew intuitively that power had gone out of him." Power [energy—in this case extraordinary energy] had gone out of him (Mark 5:30).

Thinking of prayer as either positive or negative energy is simply a theory—not a scientific fact. But it has been helpful to me in analyzing why some prayers are answered and others are not.

The most positive energy in the world is love. When someone loves us, we can actually feel their love—it is an uplifting experience. But when someone does not like us, even though they may say they do, we can "feel" their dislike—we get "bad vibes," as some would say. Hate can be generated into a room just as surely as heat blown from a furnace, and conversely there are some people so filled with the love of God that the minute they walk into a room, the atmosphere is changed. Usually, most of us live somewhere in between—not full of hate, but not full of love, either.

The apostle John tells us God is love. This isn't just a description; it doesn't mean that love is just one of the attributes of God. It is the definition of love; God is the source of love. And if our prayers are to get through to him, they must be framed in love.

Let's take an example. A missionary lived in the jungles of South America for thirty years. Every morning she got up before sunrise to spend an hour in prayer. She implored the Lord to save the souls of the "poor miserable heathen." She begged him to bring them into his kingdom and she, of course, wanted to be the instrument whereby this occurred.

She was a sinless person (after all, there was no one to sin with); she tithed; she sacrificed her life to God and to the "poor miserable heathen," and yet in thirty years she had not made a single convert.

Then one day a priest came to the area. He was one of those people from whom the love of Christ radiated. He moved among the people with ease, talking to them, getting to know them, working with them, sweating with them.

He didn't have a patronizing, sacrificial attitude; he genuinely and sincerely loved the people. They knew it; they sensed it; they responded to that love. Then, and only then, had he earned the right to tell them about the Jesus he served and knew. Soon most of the villagers had come to a knowledge of Christ—through the love of one man.

The priest also rose early in the morning to pray. But his prayers were full of positive energy. Love creates this type of energy—anything short of love means negative charges.

Why did God wait thirty years? Why didn't he work through the other missionary, even with her shortcomings? Why should the natives suffer because of her failure?

Because evidently we are the channel through which this power of God is unleashed. Just as electricity has to have power lines with which to reach its destination, so God must have us as his channels of power.

It is true he sometimes breaks the laws of the universe which he himself set up. It is true a miracle sometimes occurs without any prayer having been uttered at all (at least of which we are aware), but this is rare. The Holy Spirit resides in us as Christians, and because of this fact, he needs our participation in carrying out his plans.

Use your imagination and picture yourself the boss of an enormous construction project. You are an expert; you know what must be done and how to do it, but your workers are all amateurs; they are learning the business. If you did the work for them, they would never learn how to build. So you let them participate in the job. Every day they make mistakes, but you teach them patiently, and when the job is finished, they will each derive pride from the fact that they did their part in the building.

There are some who refuse to work. The project goes on anyway, in spite of them, but they never experience the joy of participation; they simply benefit from others' work.

You could just do the entire project yourself. If you did, it would be done right—in fact, it would be perfect. But the workers would be reduced to automatons, having had everything done for them.

Prayer is the privilege of participation. It is real communication with God. It is the knowledge that we are actually talking to Someone and he is listening. Prayer is positive energy directed toward God in the form of thoughts or words framed in love. He hears us when we tune into the right wavelength. He hears us by mental telepathy—our minds hooking up to his. We hear him when we are listening, when the channels of our minds are attuned to his.

What is prayer? It is a method of communication totally apart from any other kind. It is entering into a different dimension of space and time. It is a dialogue between lovers.

Prayer is our proof that God exists! We have the Scriptures, but if God is not a living reality in the here and now, in the nitty-gritty of today's world, then the Scriptures become nothing but a history book. It is fine to read a book and know that someone has written it, but how much more exciting that book becomes to you when you personally meet the Author!

Prayer is how we meet the Author. It is the personal touch; it is proof that we are not insignificant tiny specks on a planet millions of miles from God, who resides on a high and lofty throne. It is the knowledge that he is alive and alert and on the job. Prayer is our lifeline to the Father; without it our spiritual life is dead.

There are vast populations out there in the world who do not experience this association with God. And there are others who experience it only on a minimal level. But the only limitation is within us. Everyone can pray. The feeblest cry for help is a prayer. Prayer is entering into a privileged communication with the Creator of the universe. Kings and presidents have no more access to him than the youngest child or the poorest ditch digger. There is no rank in prayer—we are all equal.

What is prayer? It is an adventure, a never-ending one, in which we grow and learn. After the first piano lesson a student isn't ready for the concert hall; years of practice come in between. So it is with prayer. The more we pray, the more we learn about prayer, until it becomes as natural as breathing. Then, along with Paul, we can say we pray without ceasing.

Chapter II

Why Pray?

In one of the delightful tales of Narnia by C. S. Lewis, Digory complained because he and Polly had been sent on a long journey and no one had provided food for them. Fledge, their flying horse, was sure that Aslan would have done so if Digory had asked. Polly wondered if Aslan wouldn't know they needed food without their asking. "I've no doubt he would," said the horse. "But I've a sort of idea he likes to be asked" *(The Magician's Nephew)*.

Aslan, a lion, is symbolic of Christ in the Narnia tales. Lewis has a genius for explaining theology through his fictional characters.

"He likes to be asked." Over and over in the Gospels, Jesus told his disciples to ask. In the book of James we are told, "You don't get what you want because you don't ask God for it" (James 4:2). We often wish for a lot of things to happen—we hope for them—but we don't really ask for them in prayer. There is a distinct difference between wishing and asking. So this is one reason we are to pray—because the scriptures tell us to.

Why does he want us to ask? Why doesn't God just see our need and fulfill it? Because then it would be only a one-way transaction. We not only wouldn't give him the credit, we wouldn't even realize he had anything to do with the event. How could we? But if we pray and that prayer is answered, then we know who is responsible. Skeptics might call this coincidence, and perhaps in the early stages of learning to pray, we too wonder if that's not what it is. But the more we pray, and the more answers we receive from the Father, the more we realize how far from mere coincidence it is.

Corrie Ten Boom, the Dutch evangelist who was imprisoned in Ravensbruck during World War II because she hid Jews from the Nazis, told many stories of asking and receiving in her book *Tramp for the Lord*. One related how she and her sister Betsie arrived at the concentration camp by railroad car in the middle of the night. The women were lined up and forced to strip off their clothes under the watchful eyes of the prison guards. Then they entered the shower rooms where they were issued thin dresses and shoes. Corrie always carried her Bible attached to a string around her neck, concealed under her dress. She realized there would be no way to salvage her precious Bible if she had to undress in the presence of the guards.

Before she reached the head of the line, Corrie asked a guard where the toilets were. He pointed toward the shower room. Stepping out of line, she went in, quickly stuffed her Bible under a bench, and then returned to her place in line. After she had stripped and entered the shower room once more, she again hung the Bible around her neck. But now there was another problem to face. The Bible bulged under the thin dress and the women had to pass through a further inspection.

In Corrie's words: "I prayed, 'Oh, Lord, send your angels to surround us.' But then I remembered that angels are spirits and you can see through them. What I needed was an angel to shield me so the guards could not see me. 'Lord,' I prayed again, 'make your angels untransparent.' How unorthodox you can pray when you are in great need! But God did not mind. He did it. The woman ahead of me was searched. Behind me, Betsie was searched. They did not touch or even look at me. It was as though I was blocked out of their sight. Outside the building was a second ordeal, another line of guards examining each prisoner again. I slowed down as I reached them, but the captain shoved me roughly by the shoulder. 'Move along! You're holding up the line.' "

Because of this miracle Betsie and Corrie were able to hold clandestine Bible studies in the camp, bringing the message of Jesus Christ to thousands of women who had no hope.

Corrie dared to ask. Would this miracle have occurred if she hadn't? I don't know. I only know that people who do ask seem to receive so much more than those who don't. Corrie had started developing the practice of prayer years before, when there was no trouble in her life. Her daily communication with the Lord began when she was a happy, carefree youngster. Then when she needed him, when she was in trouble, they were old friends, with much in common and an abundance of trust and love in their relationship. She knew she could count on him because he had not failed her in the past.

An experience from my own life showed me the value of prayer above anything which we may try to accomplish on our own. I had been a Christian for almost a year and still could not accept all parts of the Bible as being true. This may sound strange to some, but this was an intellectual hurdle which I simply couldn't surmount.

I had been the victim of teaching which systematically demythologized the Bible. I truly did believe in the theory of evolution; I had trouble accepting the virgin birth of Christ, and I certainly didn't believe in anything as medieval as the concept of Satan. Yet I was a Christian; I had experienced Christ in my life in a very dramatic way; I knew he was real. But I wasn't growing in my faith, because growth comes from the Word of God, from reading the Bible, and letting the Holy Spirit speak to us through its pages. I did read, but my disbelief was a barrier. I was not being rebellious; I truly wanted to believe. What bothered me most was reading the words of Christ and knowing I couldn't dispute them; I knew what he said had to be true. And I knew it wasn't logical to pick and choose in the Bible;

I couldn't say one thing was true while another was not—either all of it was true or none of it was.

So I sought help. I went to counselors, preachers, and Christian friends. Each time, I argued with them about the Scriptures; I challenged them to convince me they were true. And each time I came away unsatisfied; each time I won the argument (at least in my own mind)!

Finally, one of the women to whom I had gone for help sent a young friend to see me. As I told her my problem—my inability to believe the entire Bible—she listened with interest, but much to my surprise, offered no arguments. She only said, "Let's pray about this together."

I was very new to this praying business, and uncomfortable in prayer groups where each person is expected to pray, so I immediately backed off. I explained that I really didn't like doing that sort of thing and would prefer not to, thank you. But she insisted; she was determined we were going to pray. So, much to my annoyance, we prayed—mostly she—not very much me. But I survived the ordeal, thanked her, and she left. I felt vaguely disappointed; we hadn't engaged in a good stimulating argument; she hadn't allowed me to get the better of her.

Very soon after that—and I cannot put my finger on the exact day or moment in time—I suddenly realized that I now believed the Bible to be Truth. I had no more doubts; I accepted it as the Word of God. Then I understood that what no human had been able to do with my mind, and probably never would have been able to do, the Holy Spirit had accomplished as an answer to prayer. The others from whom I sought help had not prayed with me; it had never occurred to them. The Holy Spirit accomplished supernaturally what no amount of pleading and intellectualizing had ever done.

We are so prone to give advice. Many times we are very good at seeing just what another person is doing wrong, and are sure that we are "led of the Lord" to set them straight. But more and more, I am coming to learn that what we should do for others is to pray for them.

Pray in genuine concern; pray in love; pray in confidence, and then sit back and watch God work.

We don't pray nearly enough; we have not, because we ask not. We have not good relationships with others because we don't pray about the situations—we try to take care of them ourselves. We have not the dreams of our lives because we don't pray about it.

But if God is sovereign, why pray? If our lives are predestined, and if God already knows what is going to happen, how will praying make any difference? Does prayer actually change things?

God does know everything that will happen in the future. He is not locked into our time scheme; he sees the whole plan laid out in front of him. But the fact that he knows what will happen doesn't mean he is manipulating us. We have been given free will to do as we please.

It is not that God is the author of a play in which he makes the actors say and do what he wishes; we are not puppets on a stage. At every point in life, we have the right to choose. It is just that God knows how we will choose. He has foreknowledge; he knows what we will do at any given moment in time. He knows whether or not we will pray. He knows what we will do with our lives. He has seen the script; he knows how the play will end.

The Father knew Jesus would die on the cross, and he knew when it was going to happen. But even Jesus was given free will; he could have backed out; he could have refused his assignment. Yet the Father knew he wouldn't; God could see the future and he knew Jesus would be obedient.

When we pray, we are asking God to step into our time frame, to participate with us in our particular life on Planet Earth. And although prayer does change things (that is, things would be different without prayer), the Father knows how it will all turn out. It is as if he can see the end of a movie at the same time he is seeing the beginning.

C. S. Lewis gives a vivid metaphor in his book *Miracles* that makes the connection between God's sovereignty and prayer clear to me. He compares a person's life to a black line drawn on a piece of paper. This line is conscious, but it is not conscious along its whole length at once—only at each point on that length in turn. Its consciousness, in fact, is traveling along that line from left to right, retaining point "A" only as a memory when it reaches point "B," and unable until it has left "B" to become conscious of "C." God, however, sees the whole length of the line drawn. When we pray for an event to happen at point "N," he can take into consideration all the other lines drawn on the paper and will answer the prayer accordingly.

This, you say, sounds like predestination. Not at all. Our prayer at point "N" is a part of the black line—the prayer did change things, but God knew in advance that we would pray for that event. For this reason, Lewis says our prayers can be retroactive. God sees into the future; he sees us praying and our prayers are added to others, even if we're late in expressing them.

This is a difficult concept, but one worth wrestling with, for it takes away any feelings one may have of God as being a dictatorial, rather than a loving, father.

Why are we to pray? The scriptures give us many specific reasons for prayer. There is no way to write an exhaustive list; it could go on and on, since prayer can apply to any situation. As we go through the various categories of prayer, some of the reasons will be discussed, but the best way to learn is by doing. Prayer should become an extension of breathing, a constant communication between us and our Father.

I think it is safe to say that no one exists who hasn't uttered a form of prayer at some time in his life. Probably the most universal reason for prayer is at its most basic level—a prayer for help. An avowed nonbeliever in any form of deity will cry out to "someone up there" when he finds himself unable to rely on his own or other people's resources. And in times of great physical danger, not only unbelievers, but those who know God, find themselves relying on him in a way they never had before.

Chuck and Lisa Savale are Young Life leaders in Phoenix, Arizona. In the summer of 1976, they took a group of high school students to Malibu Beyond for a one-week stress-camping situation. Beyond is north of Vancouver, British Columbia, in a setting of breathtaking beauty, of dramatic contrasts in color and form. The clear waters of the ocean inlet give way to lush green forests, cloaking mountains which rise steeply, capped by snow-covered peaks.

The camp is called Beyond not only because it is beyond the island of Malibu (where another Young Life camp is located), but because the hardships of climbing a glacier take people beyond their own resources, into reliance on God.

On this particular trip, God became a very present reality in the lives of the climbers. On the second day out from base camp, their goal was to reach the top of the ridge of Mt. Albert, 8,500 feet at its peak. The ridge is in the form of a horseshoe with a glacier rising up in the middle of this semicircle.

Under normal conditions they should have reached the top of the ridge in plenty of time to find a place to camp for the night. But soon after lunch it began to snow and sleet. The snow was very soft, making their progress slow. Their guide led the way, making a path for the others to follow—literally in his footsteps. Soon the clouds began dropping, making it harder and harder to distinguish snow from clouds, until finally they were in what is called a white-out.

Everything was white—there was no way for the guide to see the landmarks. By this time, they were all thoroughly drenched, exhausted, and hungry. They desperately needed a place to camp—a flat area—but they couldn't see to the left or right. Then the guide discovered they were on the very edge of the ridge, with a thousand-foot drop just ahead. He realized how far off course they were, and how close they had come to real danger.

They turned around and went back, but the guide was hopelessly confused. Realizing the seriousness of the situation as no one else did, he asked them to pray. He was very specific: "Pray that we will be able to see a large rock which should be on our right." So that was how they prayed—they asked God to show them the rock.

Instantly the clouds parted, and there was the rock—the very one the guide needed to see in order to know where they were! Just as quickly as it had lifted, the cloud returned; they were again surrounded by white, but they were able to walk to a level spot where they could spend the night.

Their troubles weren't over, however. A strong wind had come up, and setting up the tents became almost impossible. They were exhausted emotionally as well as physically. Two of the campers were suffering from hypothermia, a condition some mountain climbers develop when exposed to prolonged periods of cold. The body temperature is lowered to such an extent that weakness and light-headedness occur. They were shaking uncontrollably.

Finally, they were able to get one tent up, although the tent fly was torn to shreds by the wind. Ten of them huddled in that four-man tent, safe, but miserable. Just when they thought they couldn't take another catastrophe, the pole tore through the roof and the tent fell down on top of them. The only way to support the roof was to take turns holding the pole.

At that point, Chuck said, "The only thing we can do is pray." So they began. Some of them wondered why God was doing this. They questioned God's intentions—had he abandoned them up there? Were they going to make it back? Others showed their trust in him; they asked God to show them what it was he wanted them to learn.

Then Chuck said, "Let's ask God for a sign. We read all these things in the Bible about how he calms the winds and the waves; let's ask him to show us if he is really here by giving us a sign." He prayed, "Lord, if you're real, if you're here with us now in all this misery, just show us. We ask you to stop the wind."

The wind had been blowing furiously for hours. But at that moment—it stopped. They were all awe-struck, some in tears. In a very supernatural way, the Lord of the Universe answered that prayer. He showed them he was there and in control.

Although the wind did resume later, the next day dawned sunny and clear, as a much more mature group of Christians made their way back down the mountain.

Psalm 46:1, 2 puts it this way: "God is our refuge and strength, a tested help in times of trouble. And so we need not fear even if the world blows up, and the mountains crumble into the sea."

Marty Caldwell, one of the guides at Beyond, told me it is uncanny how God seems to work out the various trips. If the campers are the type who aren't used to hiking and hardships, if they probably can't stand any undue stress, then the weather is beautiful and they have an easy trip—easy by the guide's standards, but as hard as the young people on that particular trip can endure. But when the campers are able to take more, and will come through an experience like the one just described with a new understanding of their reliance on God, then something unusual always happens. They are taken "beyond."

Why pray? Because it is our lifeline to the Father. We are to pray because our Lord told us to. Corrie Ten Boom knew it; my friend who prayed with me knew it; and those young people up on the mountain learned it in a very special way. Through prayer we are taken beyond our own resources, into the realm of the heavenly kingdom.

Prayer is our key to that kingdom, but we are the ones who must turn the key.

Chapter III

Before You Pray . . .

One of the first matters to concern us in our study of prayer was the question, "Does God always hear our prayers? Are there conditions which we must fulfill before our prayers will be answered?"

Even a cursory study of prayer throughout the Bible will show many qualifications, many "ifs" at the beginning of the promises about prayer. But we seldom see those "ifs"; we scurry on to the dessert and overlook the main course.

The prayer promises must be taken within the context of each passage. Jesus was speaking to his disciples—to those who believed in him—when he gave those promises. He did not mean that the Pharisees could pray in that way—they didn't believe in Him. The same is true today. One of the first qualifications of prayer is that the extravagant promises given are meant for those who believe in Christ as being the Son of God.

Does this mean God hears only the prayers of those who have

committed their lives to Him? Not at all. But the prayer promises which are so often pulled out of context and waved around like flags, are specifically meant for believers. This distinction needs to be understood.

Beyond that, for those who do believe, there are even more conditions to be met. The following is a brief outline of what the Bible has to say about the spiritual state of the person who is praying. Isaiah 59:1, 2 reads:

> Listen now! The Lord isn't too weak to save you. And he isn't getting deaf! He can hear you when you call! But the trouble is that your sins have cut you off from God. Because of sin he has turned his face away from you and will not listen anymore.

Again in Isaiah 1:15:

> From now on, when you pray with your hands stretched out to heaven, I won't look or listen. Even though you make many prayers, I will not hear, for your hands are those of murderers.

In Jeremiah 7:16, the Lord speaks to that prophet saying:

> Pray no more for these people, Jeremiah. Neither weep for them nor pray nor beg that I should help them, for I will not listen.

Surprisingly, we see there are times when God just plain won't listen. Not only does God not hear, but we are told in Proverbs 28:9 that when one turns his ear away from the Law, his prayer is actually an abomination to the Lord.

It would be easy to explain these passages away by pointing out that they are all from the Old Testament. That was the old covenant, before Christ came; surely God no longer turns a deaf ear to a believer's prayer. But the New Testament bears the same evidence as does the Old.

In Jesus' words: "But if you live your life in me, and my words live in your hearts, you can ask for whatever you like and it will come true for you" (John 15:7). "If' we live our lives in Christ, which means being in a close relationship with him, not broken by unconfessed sin, we can ask and he will answer our prayer.

This does not mean just having a personal relationship with Christ. It means we must be currently—*now*—living in Christ. The Amplified Bible reads, "If you live in Me—abide vitally united to Me—and My words remain in you *and* continue to live in your hearts, ask whatever you will and it shall be done for you" (John 15:7).

The original Greek in which the New Testament was written has much more explicit verb tenses than does English. The tense of the word "abide" actually means "continuing to abide." I think we sometimes read this to mean "if you are a Christian, if you have given your life to him," but it is much more demanding than that. It means we must be living in Jesus right now, at the very moment we are praying.

The apostle John tells us, "We receive whatever we ask for, because we are obeying his orders and following his wishes" (I John 3:22). Another conditional promise. Peter writes more in Old Testament language when he says, "For the eyes of the Lord are upon the righteous, And his ears unto their supplication: But the face of the Lord is against them that do evil" (I Peter 3:12). And in the Gospel of John we are told, "Everybody knows that God does not listen to sinners. It is the man who has a proper respect for God and does what he wants him to do—he's the one God listens to" (John 9:31).

What does this mean? How could God not hear someone? Doesn't he know when every sparrow falls? Isn't he aware of everything that is happening at all times? Then why can't he hear?

I used to think of God as being rather obstinate. There were certain rules, and if we broke those rules, he bowed his neck, dug in his heels, and stubbornly waited for us to give in—to repent, ask forgiveness, and promise never to do it again.

But in studying these passages which speak of his not hearing us, I began to wonder if he didn't mean exactly what he said. He actually doesn't hear us; the sin in our lives creates static on the airwaves. Or

39

maybe a person's prayer doesn't even make it; maybe the negative charge makes it so weak it isn't being transmitted.

We tend to ignore these very obvious appendages to God's promises. We do not read the verses which contain prayer promises within their context. We snatch them out for our convenience, and pray, and pray, and pray, and wonder why God doesn't answer. When actually God is not even hearing us—much less answering us!

Again using Agnes Sanford's analogy of prayer as electricity, picture God as the power source and ourselves as the receptacle (a lamp, for instance), which supplies the light. If we plug a lamp into the wall socket and it does not work, we don't say to ourselves, "Well, I guess the source of power [the law of electricity] doesn't work." Instead, we look at the wiring of the lamp. We find the trouble. And when we find it and fix it, we plug it in again and it works!

So it is with our lives. There are many variables in prayer, many conditions which have to be met, but the foremost is the spiritual state of the person praying.

Therefore, the first thing we should do when we go to prayer is to examine ourselves inwardly, and then confess. To confess does not mean to tell God what we are doing; he already knows. "Confess" in the original Greek means "to agree"—we agree with God that what we are doing is sin. Then, having agreed, we give it up.

This very vital part of our relationship with the Lord has been neglected in most of the Christian denominations. Only the Roman and Anglican churches have continued the practice of confession, and even there in many instances, the importance of it is being diminished.

There are good reasons for this, since the act of confession was often abused by those who practiced it. But I can't help thinking the Protestant reformers were too extreme when they abolished confession in their churches. It is true we no longer need a mediator; Christ is our heavenly priest, and we can go directly to the Father through him. But in the book of James, we are told to confess our sins to one another. There is something very therapeutic, as well as convicting, when a person has to tell someone else the darkest secrets of his soul. It is hard to do; yet it can be a very cathartic experience.

Edith Bunker, on the television show "All in the Family," describes the confessional boxes in the Roman Catholic Church as "telephone booths to God." I think formal confession is a good institution. It isn't necessary for our friends to know all the gory details of our lives; in many cases it would wreck the friendship. But to go to a nameless and faceless intermediate and pour out our hearts is a purifying and cleansing act, one which is missing from many Christian lives.

However, confession should not be limited to a once-a-month ritual, one which is not even available to many people. Confession should be a vital part of our daily walk with God. Maybe the term "confession" should not be used—it may be a threatening word; it may connote gross sins which we don't want to admit we have.

Father John Powell, a Jesuit priest who has written many books and has valuable insights into the psychology of the soul, calls this type of praying "telling God who I am." And after we have told God who we are, we should ask him to accept us. This is not hiding in the bushes from God, as Adam tried to do. It is being open with Him. It is saying, "I don't feel like praying today," or, "I have lots of doubts about your goodness today, Lord." It is emptying ourselves of pious, meaningless phrases and just "letting it all hang out."

Prayer is the one area where we shouldn't feel threatened. It is private; no one else hears what we say; there is no worry about confidentiality. It is learning to trust God; it is being specific with him.

It is not saying, "Oh, what a worm I am," as some eighteenth-century hymns proclaim. It is saying, "I really blew it yesterday, and I'm full of bitterness and resentment, and I'm mad; but most of all, I don't like myself today, Lord." It is like a psychiatrist's couch—but it's free!

When the scriptures say God doesn't hear us, that doesn't mean he will wait until we become good persons and then he will listen. It means if we are pretending to be good when we're not, he won't hear

41

us. It means getting rid of our self-righteousness, becoming aware of how far we have missed the mark, and telling him about it. We need to tell God we are struggling. He knows all this anyway, but the prayer session is for our benefit—not his.

If you are a parent, you can identify with the problem of dealing with a child who lies. The chocolate milk is spilled all over the rug. You are angry about the milk being spilled, but what really makes you mad is that the child says he didn't do it, and you know he did. He thinks he will escape punishment by denying it, but it doesn't work that way. Instead, you are twice as angry because he didn't have the courage to admit his mistake. If he would come to you and say, "Gee, I'm sorry I spilled the milk; let me help you clean it up," the whole picture would change.

Some of us may rebel against the word "sin." Why don't we like it? I guess because it is so condemnatory. We would rather say "mistakes," but the trouble is that some of our mistakes are pretty well-planned.

Jesus had much to say about sin, and sometimes his definition of sin surprised his followers who had been steeped in the Pharisaic tradition of rules upon more rules.

Jesus interpreted sin as being inner attitudes and motives, not outward appearances, or the breaking of religious laws. In Mark we read:

> Can't you see that anything that goes into a man from outside cannot make him "common" or unclean? You see, it doesn't go into his heart, but into his stomach, and passes out of the body altogether, so that all food is clean enough. But, whatever comes out of a man, that is what makes a man "common" or unclean. For it is from inside, from men's hearts and minds, that evil thoughts arise—lust, theft, murder, adultery, greed, wickedness, deceit, sensuality, envy, slander, arrogance and folly! All these evil things come from inside a man and make him unclean! (Mark 7:18-23)

The basic nature of sin is self-assertiveness in relation to God. It is going our own way, "doing our own thing." That was what happened in the Garden of Eden, and that is what happens everytime we go against God's will. Jesus made it clear that the degree of sin isn't what is really important; what matters are our inner motives.

Recently a dust storm sprang up suddenly in the late afternoon. I ran out to roll up the windows of the car. By the time I had three of the four windows up, the wind was really fierce, and I was tempted just to forget the fourth window. "Oh, well, most of the dust will stay out of the car," I told myself. But the problem with that kind of reasoning is that the car wouldn't be really clean. It might not get as much dust inside as if all the windows were open, but there still would be dust; the car still would be dirty inside.

So it is with sin. It isn't important how *much* dust is in our lives; we need to keep *all* the windows rolled up.

Then why bother to pray? No one is perfect—who will be heard?

This takes us back to the first chapter where we defined prayer. Prayer isn't just asking. The verses about unanswered prayer have to do with asking God for something. If we are going to *ask,* we must fulfill these conditions; we have to clean up our act.

But if we just want to *talk* to God, spend time thrashing something out; or better yet, if we want to dwell on all the good things he has done for us, that's different. God will hear us. These verses don't say he won't. But it takes us so long to realize that God is just. Although he is merciful, he cannot overlook sin as if it weren't there—it must be judged.

This is so important for new Christians to learn. Often they are shown the prayer promises and they go forth with great excitement to test out this new power in prayer. And often they are disappointed. It all comes from seeing only those parts of the Bible which we want to see and pretending the rest isn't there. This is childish; we must go on to a more mature understanding of prayer.

The scriptures do give us some specific references to sins which keep our prayers from being answered.

In Peter's first epistle, he writes that husbands must try to understand their wives, honoring them as the physically weaker sex, yet equal heirs to the grace of life, *in order that they will be able to pray together properly* (I Peter 3:7). This does not say God doesn't hear, but evidently there will be a blockage somewhere along the line if a husband is not treating his wife as he should.

How many active church members do you suppose might fall into this category? You know the type. On Sunday morning, he arrives early at church with his family, carrying the big, black Bible in his hand. "Good morning, good morning," he smiles.

And little Mrs. Sparrow, whose husband never comes to church, thinks, "Oh, my—I wish my husband were more like him. He is such a good man."

Yet, is he? When the door closes on the privacy of his household, is the smile gone? Are his phrases about the goodness of the Lord reserved only for the church folk? If so, probably nothing much is happening in his prayer life.

Though not quite as specific, the same epistle speaks of wives being adaptive to their husbands, and implies that God will be much more willing to answer the wives' prayers concerning their husbands' spirituality, if the wives are behaving as God would like them to.

One surprising reason for not receiving answers to prayer is greed. First John 3:17-24 speaks of people who have an abundance of the world's goods, yet who, seeing others who have too little, refuse to share. In this context, the passage goes on to say that if our consciences do not condemn us in the matter (greed), we may have confidence before God, and we will receive from him whatever we ask, because we keep his commandments and do what pleases him.

Second Corinthians speaks of this: "All I will say is that poor sowing means a poor harvest, and generous sowing means a generous harvest" (II Cor. 9:6). Then in Proverbs 21:13 it is put very bluntly: "He who shuts his ears to the cries of the poor will be ignored in his own time of need."

Another very explicit prerequisite given for prayer is forgiveness. The Lord's Prayer is so familiar to us we are not really conscious of the meaning of the words when we say, "forgive us our debts as we forgive our debtors." Some churches have changed the word "debts" to "trespasses," and others use the word "transgressions." But the word in the original Greek is "debts."

This word has the connotation of a service unrendered. It means an unfulfilled obligation (the neighbor we never have time to help; the lonely relative we will write to someday). In other words, it is not just the overt sins which we commit toward others or they toward us, it is also the sins of omission which hinder our relationships.

And notice that we also are put in the position of the neglected. We are to forgive those who neglect us; we are to forgive those who do not do unto us as we would like them to. This covers a much broader area in our lives than out-and-out wrongs which we suffer from others.

In the version as related by Matthew, Jesus goes on to say: "For if you forgive other people their failures, your heavenly Father will also forgive you. But if you will not forgive other people, neither will your Father forgive you your failures" (Matt. 6:14, 15).

We who reside in comfortable suburban homes, where people live in peace and politeness, very seldom suffer from flagrant abuse. Yet we constantly build up resentment against friends or family because of things they fail to do. We have not "forgiven them their debts to us"; we are holding resentment within ourselves—resentment which eventually turns to bitterness.

And we also in this prayer ask God to forgive us our debts to him. He is saying he will forgive us for all the times we have failed him, if we will forgive others who have failed us.

Mark 11:25 gives us a direct warning regarding forgiveness: "And whenever you stand praying, you must forgive any grudge that you are holding against anyone else, and your Heavenly Father will forgive you your sins."

Prayer is our means of asking for forgiveness, but it is not a request to be taken lightly; it isn't a one-way street. Before we are forgiven from above (vertically), we must first forgive here on earth (horizontally).

James, the brother of Jesus, wrote a letter to the Christian Jews who had fled Jerusalem because of persecution. It is a sort of manual for Christian living with many brief admonitions.

In regard to prayer, James says:

> You crave for something and don't get it; you are murderously jealous of what you can't possess yourselves; you struggle and fight with one another. You don't get what you want because you don't ask God for it. And when you do ask he doesn't give it to you, for you ask in quite the wrong spirit—you only want to satisfy your own desires. (James 4:2, 3)

We tend to think of the early church as being much more "spiritual" than we are, but it looks as if they had many of the same problems.

There are various reasons why God doesn't answer prayer. Only a thorough study through the Scriptures of this subject will give the entire picture. But it is so vital! If prayer is our way of communicating with God, and if there are reasons why God will not hear or will not answer, then we must at least be familiar with those reasons.

I have never really enjoyed football because I don't understand the complex rules—I am definitely a casual observer. But my husband watches it with keen interest because he understands it; he knows every penalty called; he recognizes superior and inferior playing. And the players on the field must know the rules of the game; they wouldn't think of going out to play without at least a rudimentary knowledge of the rules.

The trouble with any analogy is that when carried to its extreme, it breaks down. It is obvious that some cheat in football and go on to win the game—I am only using this as an illustration.

But in the game of Life, there is no cheating allowed. The Rulekeeper won't permit it. There are certain rules for the game, whether we like it or not.

A prayer is a request, and the nature of requests is that they can be either granted or denied. But if we are right with the Father, he will let us know why the request was denied—if not right away, then eventually.

But always, always, we must remember that prayer isn't a vending machine. Just putting in our dime doesn't mean the answer to a prayer will come rolling out!

Chapter IV

How to Pray

These days the bookstores are filled with how-to books. We seem to feel we must see written instructions from an expert in each field before we dare embark on a new venture.

Prayer, however, doesn't fall into the category of activities requiring step-by-step instructions. It is highly individualized, varying in different cultures and personalities. The moment we become dogmatic about forms of prayer, we lose our spontaneity and become more conscious of *how* we are praying than *what* we are praying.

This funny little poem spoofs our habit patterns which have become so ingrained they border on being gimmicks.

> "The proper way for a man to pray,"
> Said Deacon Lemuel Keyes,
> "And the only proper attitude
> Is down upon his knees."

"No, I should say the way to pray,"
Said Reverend Doctor Wise,
"Is standing straight with outstretched arms
And rapt and upturned eyes."

"Oh, no, no, no," said Elder Slow,
"Such posture is too proud.
A man should pray with eyes fast-closed
And head contritely bowed."

"It seems to me his hands should be
Austerely clasped in front
With both thumbs pointing toward the ground,"
Said Reverend Doctor Blunt.

"Last year I fell in Hidgekin's well
Headfirst," said Cyrus Brown,
"With both my heels a-stickin' up
And my head a-pointin' down.

"And I made a prayer right then and there,
The best prayer I ever said,
The prayingest prayer I ever prayed,
A-standin' on my head!"
—Sam Walter Foss
"The Prayer of Cyrus Brown"

It's true God isn't judging us by the correct wording of our prayers; he isn't listening for the right tone of voice or the proper position of our knees. But this doesn't preclude our learning more about how to pray. One of the best ways to learn is to study the prayer life of Jesus, and read what he had to say about prayer.

It must have been fun to be one of the disciples. As they walked from town to town, Jesus was constantly teaching them. Yet he never gave long, theological discourses. Instead, and many times with irrepressible humor, he would answer questions with stories rather than a yes or no. These stories are called parables, and sometimes they seem confusing. To make them as understandable to us as they were to the disciples two thousand years ago, I have loosely paraphrased and updated some of them.

Jesus seemed to have had a "thing" about long prayers in public. He hated hypocrisy and repeatedly accused the religious leaders of the day of being pretenders {hypocrite means "pretender" in Greek}. I have adapted the parable this way:

> Watch out for those religious leaders who love to be seen in public in their clerical collars and have everyone say, "Hello, Reverend. Come right in and sit on the front seat where everyone can see you; this is the section reserved for distinguished guests." They are given the best seats at banquets, right at the head table. These same men own property rented out to the poor; they are landlords of the slums; they take advantage of people, and then they try to mask their real character by saying long, beautiful prayers. But they are only making their eternal punishment worse! (Mark 12:38-40)

Many times long prayers are spoken in our worship services. In some congregations the prayers are written and are part of the ritual of the church. Often these are beautiful; the words have been carefully thought out to express the corporate desires of the people. The repetition of the ritual has a very meaningful effect on those who are accustomed to hearing it; it provides a continuity which links us to the church back through the centuries.

There is nothing wrong with these rote prayers; but what must be remembered is that, rather than prayers, they are actually acts of worship. They have their place in the service, but they should never be substitutes for real and private communication with the Father.

And as Jesus pointed out, lengthy prayers won't get us off the hook. Going to church on Sunday will not help us, if during the week we have deliberately done harm to others.

On another occasion, Jesus illustrated the importance of our inner motives when we pray. Today, he might tell the story this way:

> Two men went to the church to pray. One was a minister; the other was a member of the Mafia. The minister stood and prayed (not to God, he was really talking to hear himself talk): "O God, I thank you because I am such a perfect person—not like everyone else and especially not like

51

that gangster over there (by the way, how did he get in here?). I give away ten percent of everything I make (and I want everyone to know about it). I never steal; I never think bad thoughts; money isn't important to me (as long as I have enough); and most of all, I go without food twice a week (so that others will know I'm religious)."

But the guy from the Mafia didn't feel very welcome in the church and he stood in a dark corner, hoping no one would notice him. He was so aware of how bad he was that he didn't even know if he could pray. He barely raised his eyes in a defeated gesture, and said, "God, please help me. I know I'm a sinner!"

The story over, Jesus might go on to explain, "I assure you, that gangster is the one whom the Lord looked upon with his infinite mercy, rather than the minister. Because everyone who thinks he is something special is really nobody, and everyone who realizes how much he needs God and is sorry for things he has done, will become someone very special in God's eyes" (Luke 18:10-14).

We all hate self-righteousness, and yet we are all guilty of it to some degree. Richard Nixon had no part in the Watergate burglary; it was the coverup and his subsequent denial of the coverup which were his downfall. His self-righteous attitude in the light of later revelations lost him the respect of the nation.

In Psalm 51:17 we are told that the Lord loves a broken and contrite spirit. Why? Because it is at this point that he can begin to work in our lives. Otherwise, like the religious leader in the above passage, we are filled with pride—pride of what *we* have done, with no reliance upon God.

When studying the prayer habits of Jesus, one is impressed with the fact that he almost always went off by himself to pray. The only exception to this was his great intercessory prayer for the apostles which is related in John's Gospel. Again and again, the scriptures speak of Jesus as being alone when he prayed. The night before he chose the twelve apostles, he spent the entire night in prayer—alone. After his baptism by John, he spent forty days and nights in the wilderness—alone in prayer.

He never held a prayer meeting. He never said, "All right, Peter, why don't you start and we'll pray around the group, and in a few minutes I'll close." Even when he took some of the apostles with him, he was always by himself while actually praying.

Often when we pray in a group, what we really are doing is performing for one another. As others are praying, we are hastily making up what we are going to say, and we barely listen to the others' prayers. We carefully phrase our prayer so as to impress the others in our prayer circle.

Jesus might have said this:

> When you pray, don't pretend to be an actor on the stage. Don't pray with the motive of having others see and hear you. All these actors want is praise from the people who see them, and believe me, that's all they're going to get. But when you pray, do it in the privacy of your own home, in your own room, alone with the Father. The Father will see you and he will reward you for being sincere. And don't think that because you know how to say long, beautiful prayers it will do you any good. (Matt. 6:5-7)

Then why do we pray in groups? Why did the disciples pray together after Jesus left them to go to the Father? Because Jesus promised that where two or three were gathered together in his name, he would be there also. And he gave them the promise that if two of them agreed to ask for anything, the Father would give it to them.

Obviously, he is not telling us to pray alone all the time. There are places for both types of prayer in our lives. As is always true with Jesus' teachings, the motive is the important thing. The person in the above parable wasn't *praying with* others—he was *performing for* them. There is a difference.

Jesus' words are clear—more power is released when two people pray (in agreement) than when one prays alone. Why? Why should it matter whether or not we agree on a request, and why is there more power when two or more pray together?

Thinking of God as being president of the board will help us understand how this works. As president, he has more than 50 percent of the stock; he has full control of the decisions. But the way the bylaws are written, the other members of the board have voting rights; they are allowed to have their say when there is a decision to be made. If their desires are in the best interests of the corporation, and if there is a majority pulling for a certain result, the president will be more likely to consider the request.

If there is not full agreement, there is friction. Negative energy is being thought, if not spoken. But when two believers are really sincere, and are united in their petition, the power of their positive energy (love) is generated to the Father, allowing him to work without hindrance.

If a minister is praying for a congregation and the people are not in agreement with what he is saying, his prayer is seriously hampered. The negative thoughts work against his prayer and the power has trouble being transmitted.

In Acts 2:1-4, we are told that the disciples were together, *in one accord,* when the Holy Spirit descended upon them. They were not having a church meeting where everyone had a different opinion about the issues. They were praying together, in total agreement. The full power of their combined prayers was going to the Father.

Group prayer is very important, but there are pitfalls. Our motives must be right; we must be united in our desire for the petitions, and if we are only performing, then we may as well forget it. God doesn't need any present-day Pharisees.

Rosalind Rinker is noted for her books and seminars on prayer. It is a frustrating experience, however, to attend her lectures because one has only four hours to listen to her and wishes it were four days—she is such a delightful person!

Her suggestions deal mainly with conversational prayer in small groups. And when she says small, that is exactly what she means. She believes any group larger than four is detrimental to togetherness. If there are five people present, two should split off to form their own small group.

She suggests using a structured order in our small-group prayer sessions. This is shown here as described in her book, *Conversational Prayer*.

"1. Jesus Is Here—The Power of Worship"

First become aware that Jesus is with you, in the prayer circle. He promised he would be. Dwell on that for a moment either silently or verbally.

"2. Thank You, Lord—The Power of Thanksgiving"

Verbalize the things you are grateful for. Be specific.

"3. Help Me, Lord—The Power of Confession"

Don't confess for someone else—only for yourself! This is not a time for divulging deep, dark secrets; it is a time to ask for help with problems, decisions.

"4. Help My Brother—The Power of Intercession"

Pray for the requests the others in the group have expressed.

We so often go straight to Step Four in our prayer groups, without considering the other areas of prayer.

Rosalind suggests thinking of prayer as a ball which bounces back and forth from person to person in the group. One subject is prayed about at a time. For example, when one person prays for help in some area of his life, the others in the group intercede for that person before the Lord. It would go something like this:

1st person: Lord, help me to like my neighbor—she just makes me so mad!

2nd person: Yes, Lord, I also ask you to help Betty understand her neighbor.

3rd person: Lord, I hold Betty up to you in holy intercession. I agree with her in this prayer and ask you to help her.

4th person: Lord, I understand what Betty is going through. I have had the same problem with a neighbor of mine. Please help her as you did me.

Then the group can go on to another subjct. This will involve all the members of the prayer circle in each person's prayer. They must listen; they must really care about every person's request. The same sequence is carried out in each step. Everyone doesn't have to pray each time, of course. But there is an opportunity for all to pray if they wish.

One other important suggestion is that we touch each other during the prayer time, either by holding hands or by putting our arms around one another—a physical touch. Something very powerful happens in a group when we are able to let down our inhibitions and show other persons we care enough to touch them.

Group prayer, however, just like worship, should not take the place of personal prayer. Only there can things be said which we would never discuss in a group. Only there, alone, can we give God our full attention.

Sometimes we are uncertain whether we should pray over and over about something, or whether this would signify doubt, and because of our lack of faith, the prayer would not be answered. A closer look at the scriptures will show that we are to pray again and again for the same thing and that doing this does not in any way show a lack of faith.

The disciples also wondered about repeated prayer and asked Jesus about it. As usual, he didn't give them just a yes-or-no answer. He told them a story something like this:

> Once upon a time, there was a mean, cruel judge. He didn't believe in God and wasn't afraid of anyone. Now, there was a poor defenseless widow in that town, and she kept asking the judge for protection from a man who was about to foreclose on her mortgage and drive her out into the cold. For a long time, the mean old judge refused. But finally he thought to himself, "It's true that I'm mean, and I don't believe in God, and I'm not afraid of anyone, but this dad-blamed woman is about to drive me crazy! I'll have to settle this case in her favor or else she will be the death of me with her constant nagging!"
>
> Then Jesus might have said, "If this judge, who was not holy or moral, finally gave in because of the widow's persistence, don't you think the Father will see that justice is done?" (Luke 18:1-7)

This parable is often misunderstood. God is not being compared to the mean judge; he is being contrasted to him. The judge is symbolic of all the evil and cruelty which mankind perpetrates upon itself. The widow symbolizes all the poor—all the people used by the others who are in power. What Jesus is saying is that if the poor can obtain what they need from the abusive powers on earth, how much more will their Father in heaven give them what they need, if they will only ask?

Would anyone pray only once and then stop, if their child were seriously ill? No one would pray, "Please make Johnny well," on the first day of his illness and then never mention it again. We would pray constantly for him.

The Gospel according to Luke tells us the story of Elizabeth and Zacharias who were "getting on in years" as Luke puts it, and had no child. In the Jewish tradition, to be childless was a disgrace. It was especially humiliating to be a priest of the tribe of Aaron and to die with no descendants. One day when Zacharias was burning incense in the temple, an angel appeared to him with a message. "Your prayers have been heard. Elizabeth your wife will bear you a son, and you are to call him John" (Luke 1:13, 14).

"Your prayers have been heard . . ." This wasn't the first time Zacharias had prayed. He and his wife had prayed for a child for many years. They did not pray once and stop; they asked, and asked, and asked. And their prayers were answered.

Jesus tells us to ask, to seek, to knock. This is an ongoing process; we are to be continually asking, seeking, and knocking. One helpful interpretation is to think of this kind of prayer as cumulative. In other words, when we pray over and over for the same thing, we are not saying, "I know you might have forgotten about this, Lord, so I'm reminding you." What we are doing is simply adding prayer upon prayer. We are showing by our consistent prayers that we mean business; we are really concerned about our petition. We do not lose heart; we don't give up easily.

Jesus told another parable similar to the one about the evil judge. In Luke 11:6, 7, this parable immediately follows the Lord's prayer, which was given to the disciples when they asked Jesus to teach them to pray.

In an updated form, he might tell them:

> What if your mother-in-law arrived in the middle of the night (she hadn't written to say she was coming) and she was hungry and you didn't have a thing in the house to eat. So you went over to your neighbor's house and began knocking on the door. Bang! Bang! Bang! You knew they were asleep, so you knocked extra loud so they would wake up. The neighbor yelled down, "Don't bother me; the door is locked, and we are all in bed, and I don't want to get up."

Jesus went on to explain that even if the neighbor wouldn't get up and give him some bread out of the goodness of his heart, he would do so just to stop the noise, so he could go back to sleep.

In this parable Jesus was telling us that we should pray again and again. The next verse is the one in which he tells us to ask and seek and knock.

I once heard a radio evangelist tell the story of being very ill when he was scheduled for a large meeting. He didn't know how he could possibly get through the meeting, yet he knew he must not fail all those people. So he knelt by the side of his bed and prayed for healing. Nothing happened. Again, he asked the Lord to take away his illness. Nothing happened. He persisted; he kept on praying. He claimed he actually prayed the same prayer 529 times! And on the 529th time he was "instantly" healed! God certainly knew that evangelist was sincere in his prayer. He didn't give up, and not only was he healed, but he learned a valuable lesson about prayer.

One of the most helpful tools for effective prayer is visualization. We each visualize God in a different way, but I have found that most people visualize Jesus, rather than the Father, when they pray. We are unable to conceive in our imaginations what the Father looks like. This is fine; Jesus said whoever had seen him had seen the Father.

A friend told me she always imagines Jesus as a shepherd. She sees him in a field with a staff in his hand and when she prays, she sees herself in his arms.

Another friend spoke of how she imagines herself walking out of her town, past the school, past her husband's work, past her house, past all her earthly concerns. She meets Jesus in a field with daisies scattered about, and she comes to him and sits on his knee.

When these stories were told to me, my reaction was to wince a bit. I thought that was fine for them, but it sounded a little too cloying. Then the Lord gave me my due comeuppance. As I began trying to visualize Jesus before I prayed, I involuntarily saw him in the same field my friend had described. But I only stood before him. Then in my mind's eye and much to my surprise, he came over to me and put his arms around me! If we won't humble ourselves and go to him, he will come to us.

This is a highly individual thing, but it does work. It helps us to concentrate, to make our conversations with the Lord more real.

How we actually pray isn't important. Jesus is only mentioned once in the Bible as kneeling in prayer. In fact, most of the time he was standing up with his eyes wide open, looking up toward heaven. At other times he prayed lying flat on the ground. As the little poem at the beginning of the chapter points out, it is a purely personal matter.

Throughout the Bible there is mention of hands uplifted in prayer, a practice which is coming back with the charismatic renewal. It is difficult to drop our inhibitions and try it for the first time, but once accustomed to it, it can be a very meaningful form of worship.

When we pray isn't important either. It is good to start the day with prayer, even if it is only a hasty, "Good morning, Lord." As with anything, our true intention is what matters. Do we care enough about our Lord to spend a definite portion of our day with him? We may say we talk to God all day, but it isn't the same as that private, set-aside time.

"Marriage Encounter," a weekend retreat for married couples, teaches what they call a "ten and ten." Twenty minutes of dialogue with your mate each day: ten minutes of telling your own thoughts and feelings; ten minutes of listening to your mate. A "ten and ten" with the Lord every day will improve the relationship, just as it does in marriage.

We all have trouble finding time to pray. It seems no matter how often we vow to get up a half hour earlier, the alarm doesn't go off and the time is gone. Once our day begins, there is never a half-hour slot which we can set aside just to be with the Lord. I am the chief sinner among you—there is no way I could throw the first stone. But something happened one day which led me to a deeper understanding of prayer.

I was having an unusually busy day because we were hosting a large meeting at our house that evening. Suddenly, around two o'clock, I realized I had not prayed at all that day.

Then came the little argument with myself, "You don't have time to sit down to pray; just pray right here in the kitchen—God will understand." But something told me to drop everything and go have a quiet time with the Lord.

He spoke to me during that prayer time. He told me I was actually sacrificing time to pray. I was giving some of my time to make it his time, and he told me he valued that sacrifice highly. I realized that if I had nothing to do all day and spent a half hour with him, it wouldn't be nearly so precious to him as if I gave up some urgently needed time for him.

The principle of sacrifice is found all through the scriptures. In Romans 12:1, Paul says, "With eyes wide open to the mercies of God (which means realizing how grateful we should be to God for forgiving us all we've done against him), I beg you, my brothers, as an act of intelligent worship, to give him your bodies, as a living *sacrifice,* consecrated to him and acceptable by him." What we do with our time is what we do with our bodies. God wants us to pray whether it is a sacrifice or not. But for most of us, it is a sacrifice of time; there is always something else which we need or want to do.

The Creator has given each of us the same amount of time each day, whether we are the President of the United States or a two-year-old child. We all have twenty-four hours. How we spend that time is up to us—we choose. If one wishes to watch soap operas for two hours a day, that is his prerogative, but it is pretty hard to justify the statement, "I don't have time," later in the day.

Christ said, "Let him deny himself, and take up his cross and follow me" (Matt. 16:24 KJV). Deny yourself a television program; deny yourself a phone call, a nap, whatever you wish. Deny yourself, and give that time to God in prayer. The sacrifice is small—the reward great.

Usually the last phrase in our prayers is, "In Jesus' name we pray," or some variation of these words. And this is as it should be; we are told by Jesus to pray in his name. "I assure you that whatever you ask the Father he will give you in my name. Up to now you have asked nothing in my name; ask, and you will receive, that your joy may be overflowing" (John 16:24). Praying in Jesus' name is our card of authority. It is like an engraved invitation which we are required to show before entering a gala event. It is our badge which says, "The prayer promises are for me, because I am a believer."

But of course, the Father knows whether or not we are believers. So just tacking the words "In Jesus' name" onto a prayer is useless unless we really mean it. There is no way to pray in Jesus' name if we have doubts about his diety, and there is no way to pray in his name if the request is something we know is wrong. Therefore, we should not take the phrase lightly.

Praying in Jesus' name isn't a gimmick; it isn't a magic formula to have our prayers answered. Rather, it reveals an attitude—an inner obedience to something Jesus told us to do; a fresh awareness of his power, of who he is. It is saying, "Father, I'm asking this not because I am worthy, but because Jesus Christ died for me and he gave me the authority to pray in his name."

Chapter V

The Prayers of Jesus

Long before Jesus' time, the philosopher Aristotle made famous the peripatetic method of teaching. Rather than sitting in a classroom, the pupils "walked around" with their teacher. That is what the word "peripatetic" means. They followed him, and he taught them as the circumstances arose, using object lessons.

That is the manner in which the apostles learned. At times they listened when Jesus spoke in the synagogue. But most of the time they were walking around on the hillsides, by the Sea of Galilee, through the dusty streets. And as questions came up, they were taught by the Master. Much of his teaching was about prayer.

Jesus was a great storyteller. He was ebullient and full of the joy of life. I think he enjoyed being here on earth very much, even though he certainly didn't have an easy life. He loved people and loved being with them. He had an especially strong attachment toward his apostles, who were with him night and day.

Matthew 21:21, 22, tells us of the time Jesus was returning to Jerusalem after having spent the night in Bethany. It was early in the morning and he was hungry. He saw a fig tree growing by the side of the road, but when he came to it, he discovered there was nothing on it but leaves. "No more fruit shall ever grow on you!" he said to it (yes, he spoke to the fig tree). Immediately, the fig tree withered away, much to the amazement of the disciples. "How on earth did you do that?" they asked.

I can just picture Jesus walking on at a fast pace, with the disciples panting to catch up. With wide gestures of his arms showing his wild, free spirit, Jesus answered, "Believe me, if you have faith and have no doubts in your heart, you will not only do this to a fig tree, but even if you should say to this hill, 'Be uprooted and thrown into the sea,' it will happen! Everything you ask for in prayer, if you have faith, you will receive."

He so wanted them to share his enthusiasm; he wanted them to capture his vision; he wanted them to realize their full potential.

How very far from that kind of power we have come today. "Everything" you ask for in prayer "if" you have faith—but how few of us do have that kind of faith. We think we do; we can all quote instances of absolute faith, but if we are honest and analyze our true feelings, we can't pass the test of the words, "and have no doubts in your heart." We do have doubts.

I enjoyed the movie production of *Godspell* so much because Jesus was portrayed as a young man, bursting with energy and happiness, wanting to share the good news with everyone. His only sorrow came when there were some who would not receive what he had come to give.

Jesus certainly did not pray just to be an example to the apostles. He obviously needed to pray. We are not told specifically that he rose to pray early *every* morning, but the implication is there—it is mentioned so often. Whenever he had a difficult decision to make or when the crowds became too large, he slipped away by himself to pray. It is true that he and the Father were one; he had constant communion with him. But he still needed those times of complete concentration to speak to the Father.

Why did Jesus pray at all? If he was in constant touch with the Father, why did he need to go off by himself to pray? If one of us were given only three years to bring a new and revolutionary message to the world, we would not waste valuable time in prayer! We would get on with it, working like beavers every minute.

But Jesus seemed to need to pray. He was evidently praying for guidance. He was somewhat like a spy in enemy territory who needed to check with headquarters for vital information and orders. His life was in danger; he walked a tightrope between defying the religious leaders who wanted to get rid of him, and getting his message to the greatest number of people possible. From the things he said on several occasions, he evidently was praying constantly for his disciples, too. Intercessory prayer was a definite part of Jesus' prayer life.

The story of Lazarus gives us a glimpse of how Jesus prayed. Lazarus and his sisters, Mary and Martha, were very close to Jesus; he stayed in their home on his way to Jerusalem.

Mary and Martha sent an urgent message to Jesus when Lazarus became ill. They knew Jesus could heal him, and they were certain he would come quickly. But he didn't. After he received the message, he deliberately put off his return to Bethany for two days. When he finally arrived, Lazarus had been dead for four days.

After speaking with the sisters, and so empathizing with their grief that he wept, Jesus asked to be taken to the grave. A large group of people were there, having come from Jerusalem to comfort the family. Jesus requested that the stone be moved from the mouth of the cave where Lazarus' body had been placed.

Jesus had not delayed coming to Bethany just because he was preoccupied with other things. He had asked for guidance from the Father as to what he should do and he had carried out the Father's orders. He knew that the miraculous event which was to take place would bring a great many people to believe in him as the Son of God.

Jesus raised his eyes toward heaven and said: "Father, I thank you that you have heard me. I know that you always hear me, but I have said this for the sake of these people standing here so that they may believe that you have sent me" (John 11:42).

Jesus had obviously been praying about Lazarus those four days. He knew the Father heard him; since he was in unbroken fellowship with the Father, he knew the Father always heard him.

You might protest that we are different; we are not divine and therefore our prayers might not always get the same results his did. But at the end of his ministry on earth, Jesus promised the apostles they would do mightier things than even he had done—if they believed.

What we learn from this story is that Jesus did not just decide to ask the Father to raise Lazarus from the dead and then sit back in total faith to watch it happen. Jesus had been seeking God's guidance for several days. When Lazarus came back to life, it was all according to the plan which the Father had conceived from the beginning; Jesus was merely his instrument. In total obedience, Jesus carried out the will of the Father, which he had previously sought through prayer.

Jesus' prayers certainly were never rote. For him, prayer was a time of deep communion with his Father. One such instance is related by Luke:

> Jesus took Peter, James and John and went off with them to the hill-side to pray. And then, while he was praying, the whole appearance of his face changed and his clothes became white and dazzling. Suddenly, two men could be seen talking with Jesus. They were Moses and Elijah—revealed in heavenly splendour, and their talk was about the way he must take and the end he must fulfil in Jerusalem. But Peter and his companions had been overcome by sleep and it was as they struggled into wakefulness that they saw the glory of Jesus and the two men standing with him. (Luke 9:28-33)

This was no ordinary prayer. Jesus was in such deep communion with the Father that he was actually changed in appearance, much the same way Moses' face shone when he came down from Mt. Sinai, after having been with the Lord. Jesus was in such direct contact with heaven that Moses and Elijah came to speak with him.

This was a crucial time in Jesus' earthly ministry. It was just before the events which led to the crucifixion. He desperately needed guidance—assurance that the steps he was taking were the right ones. And the means he used to find this guidance was prayer.

Peter, James, and John were awestruck. While they were still talking about what they had seen, a cloud overshadowed them and actually enveloped them. Then a voice came out of the cloud saying, "This is my Son, my chosen! Listen to him" (Luke 9:35). The Father instructed us to listen to Jesus just as Jesus listened to the Father—through prayer.

The location of this episode is called the Mount of Transfiguration because Jesus' appearance changed. We now say we have mountaintop experiences, times when we feel very close to the Lord. These are rare, but are unforgettable when they occur.

Mary, a friend since the days when we both had very small children, found herself facing divorce after fifteen years of marriage. It was during this time of loneliness and uncertainty that she came into a vital, personal relationship with the Father through Jesus Christ. And many times during those days of indecision and depression, she was comforted by the knowledge that Someone loved her very much.

But one night his presence became even more vividly real as she drove home from a Bible-study group where she had been sharing her problems. She was feeling especially low; the situation was becoming increasingly hard to deal with, and she was finding it difficult to keep her spirits up in front of her children. As Mary neared her house, alone in the car, with the street pitch black, she suddenly felt a hand resting lightly on her right shoulder. She should have been frightened, but at the exact moment the weight of the hand was felt, she heard the Lord say, "Everything is going to be all right."

He was there with Mary in that car, reaching out to touch her in her hour of need. That was a turning point for her in her struggle to survive. From then on, Mary had no doubt that God would protect her and guide her. It seems when we are at our lowest point, the Father lifts us up to the mountaintop to be with him. Jesus was transfigured, and sometimes we are transfigured (changed) too. Sometimes we are able to have such complete communion with God that there is a turning point in our lives.

When the disciples asked Jesus to teach them to pray, he answered by giving them a model prayer, one which has come to be called the Lord's Prayer. The familiar words are part of nearly all church services. Because they are so well known, we do not really listen to them, and they have largely lost their meaning for us. But it was not meant to become a rote prayer that we recite in church; it was meant as a framework upon which to hang all our prayers. It should be used in the same way we use a road map. We try to stay on the main road, but every single rock and tree isn't shown for us. We are free to stop or stray or take a side road; the road map is a guide to keep us from becoming hopelessly lost.

William Barclay, famed Scottish Bible scholar, makes an interesting comment on the purpose of the Lord's Prayer in his book *The Gospel of Matthew.* He says the first three petitions have to do with God and the glory of God, thereby putting God in his proper place—first. The second three petitions have to do with our needs. Dividing these separately to examine them, he points out that first we ask for bread, which is a present need. Then we ask for forgiveness, which is a need arising from the past. Third, we seek help in resisting temptation, which is a future need.

Going further, he states this is a prayer which brings the whole of our lives into the presence of God. It is also a prayer which brings the whole of God into our lives. When we ask for bread, we ask God the Father, who is the creator and sustainer of all life. When we ask for forgiveness, we ask it of Jesus, who is our Savior. And when we ask for help in facing future temptation, we ask it of God the Holy Spirit, who is the Comforter, the Strengthener, and who is here with us now.

To quote Barclay, "In the most amazing way this brief second part of the Lord's Prayer takes the present, the past, and the future, the whole of man's life, and presents them to God the Father, God the Son and God the Holy Spirit, to God in all his fullness. In the Lord's Prayer Jesus teaches us to bring the whole of life to the whole of God, and to bring the whole of God to the whole of life."

As an interesting experiment, take the words of the Lord's Prayer, and wherever there is a plural pronoun, change it to the singular. "*My* Father"; "give *me my* daily bread"; "forgive *me*." It is amazing how quickly this becomes no longer an impersonal rote prayer, but a very meaningful exercise in dialogue with the Father. Better yet, after each phrase of the prayer, stop and meditate on the meaning. What does it mean for God to be *my* Father? "Forgive me for _____." "Keep me from the temptation of _____." See if the prayer doesn't come alive with new meaning and purpose.

Jesus knew what he was doing when he gave that prayer to the disciples. And I am sure they understood that the prayer was simply a structure within which to work. But over the years, we have dimmed the light of his purpose until we can no longer see it clearly.

One of the last examples we have of the prayer life of Jesus took place in the Garden of Gethsemane the night he was arrested. Jesus went there often. The fact that Judas knew where he would be when he brought the authorities, shows it was a frequent place of prayer for Jesus. He knew what was coming and he wanted to be in private communion with his Father one last time.

He took Peter, James, and John with him. These were the same three who had accompanied him on the Mount of Transfiguration. He wanted companionship. When we are troubled, we want to know others care. But as is so often true with friends, the apostles let him down. He asked them to watch and to pray, but they fell asleep. The happenings of the previous three days had totally exhausted them.

Luke's account of the prayer of Gethsemane reads:

> "Father, if you are willing, take this cup away from me—but it is not my will, but yours, that must be done." Then he got to his feet from his prayer and walking back to the disciples, he found them sleeping

through sheer grief. "Why are you sleeping?" he said to them. "You must get up and go on praying that you may not have to face temptation." (Luke 22:44-46)

Jesus knew what crucifixion was; he had seen others die in that manner. In his humanness, he was frightened—he didn't want to suffer pain. Yet he knew he must, and he knew why he must.

But before he actually went through it, he needed to talk to the Father. He needed reassurance, guidance, comfort. He called the Father "Abba," a word which he never before had used in addressing God. "Abba" is the word a small child would use. It is the equivalent of "Daddy" and shows an intimate relationship, implying the trust of a child in his father.

And when he had finished praying, his concern was for his men. He told them to pray that they would not have to undergo a similar fate, a similar test.

Because Christ suffered as a man, he is truly our brother. He understands when we hurt. He hears us when we pray and he sits on the right hand of the Father, interceding for us.

Chapter VI

Intercessory Prayer

Picture a courtroom. The judge looks down from his high bench, which gives him a visible as well as a symbolic air of authority. The defendant sits behind a table on the floor of the courtroom. On an intermediate level stands the attorney who is pleading the case for his defendant. In eloquent words, he speaks of the merits of his client. He explains the events, and the reasons for their occurrence. He appeals to the mercy of the court. The defendant could go to trial without a lawyer if he chose; he could defend his own case, and people often do. But usually a person will fare better if an attorney intercedes for him.

Intercessor. Go-between. Middleman. That is who we are when we pray for another. We are the middleman between that person and the Father, just as Christ is the mediator for us. The Scriptures imply that this is Jesus' main occupation now—being the Advocate (lawyer) for us.

That we are also to be a part of this "ministry of the interior" was shown dramatically in the life of Janice Malone, a widow living in Maryland.

Janice's daughter Julie had been gone from home two years since graduating from high school, and there were long periods of time when Janice did not hear from her. Julie is a person who is extremely kind to everyone, picking up stray dogs, cats, and people, whenever they cross her path. Christ had not yet become real to her—Christianity was just a religion—but she did believe in the power of prayer, and she knew that wherever she was, her mother was surrounding her with that power.

One night Janice awakened with a strange sense of foreboding. She described it as having chills from the top of her head to the bottoms of her feet. It was not only that she didn't feel well; it was more than that. It was as if something evil was happening—yet she didn't know what.

As she lay there, wide awake and trying to understand the meaning of this feeling, she remembered she had been dreaming about her mother, who had been dead for several years. In the dream, her mother entered the room and knelt down beside the bed, without speaking. Janice felt she should kneel and pray with her, so she got out of bed and together they prayed—silently. Then her mother rose and walked to the door. Janice told her it had been good to see her, and opened the door for her. She left, still not speaking.

As Janice pondered the dream, she remembered how close her mother had been to Julie and she realized the dream must have meant that she should pray for Julie. The oppressive sense of something wrong was still present.

She got out of bed and knelt just as she had done in her dream. She asked the Father to surround Julie with his angels, to guard and protect her. Finally she told him she had done all she could and asked him to take over—she placed Julie in his hands. Crawling back into bed, she fell asleep instantly and awoke in the morning feeling well and at peace.

Two days later, the phone rang in the middle of the afternoon. It was Julie.

"Mama, something has happened, but don't worry, I'm all right," she began.

"What's wrong?" Janice asked anxiously.

"There was an accident," Julie said. "But I'm okay. I wasn't hurt at all, but my car was wrecked."

"How did it happen?"

"Well, two guys were with me; Jack was in the front seat and Lonnie was in the back. A man in the car behind us fell asleep at the wheel and he ran right into us.

"The whole car was torn up. Lonnie was thrown into the front with us and all our luggage and stuff in the back was crushed. But what's so strange about it is what I did while it was happening. It was as if my hands were glued to the wheel—I couldn't seem to take them off. We crossed over the median and then went clear back to the other side of the road and it seemed like we were going to turn over for sure, but we didn't. Then we went onto the median again and then back over to the side before we finally stopped. And all the time I just kept my hands on that steering wheel for dear life.

"The state trooper said he had never seen anything like it—we all should have been killed. But except for a little cut on Jack's forehead, we didn't have a scratch, and neither did the man who hit us."

Janice breathed a prayer of thanksgiving. Now she knew why she had been awakened in the night to pray. Why she was to pray twenty-four hours in advance of the accident, she didn't know. But there was no doubt in her mind that her intercessory prayer had guarded that car and kept her daughter and the others safe.

Examples of intercessory prayer are found everywhere throughout scripture, and a thorough study of these examples leads to a greater understanding of its importance.

The book of Job is said to be the oldest book in the Bible. In the last chapter, Job is instructed to pray for his friends in order to save them from God's wrath. Job 42:8 reads in part, "And my servant Job will pray for you, and I will accept his prayer on your behalf, and won't destroy you as I should because of your sin, your failure to speak rightly concerning my servant Job."

This indicates that God needs our intercessory prayers in order to serve justice and mercy at the same time. Job's two friends had sinned, and sin must be punished, or God would not be just. But if there is an intercessor, a person who is pure and sinless, then the sin will be covered over, atoned for, and mercy given.

This is what Christ did for us on the cross. He was a substitute for our sins. When we appropriate (claim for ourselves) that substitution, then we experience forgiveness just as Job's friends did.

That we can actually pray for forgiveness for others is borne out many places in scripture. James 5:14-16 tells us to pray for one another for healing as well as for forgiveness of sins. In the First Letter of John we are told to pray for brothers whom we know are committing sin. Here again, the spiritual condition of the person praying (the intercessor) matters a great deal. These verses go on to say that tremendous power is made available through a good man's earnest prayer.

Another example of this is given in Moses' life. The Lord was angry with the Israelites for making the golden calf; he threatened to break his covenant with them and begin a new nation with Moses as its founder. Moses pleaded for his people; he begged God to change his mind. His prayer was answered; God did change his mind.

At first glance this incident seems incongruous. It seems to demean God, by showing how one small person here on earth can manipulate him. But look at it another way. Think of the degree of participation which the Lord grants us! We are given important roles in the affairs of history, in other people's lives. That isn't man controlling God; it is his design to let us be a part of his plan, an active voice in the universe.

Think again of God as president of the board. We are members of the board and each of us is given the opportunity to speak. The president listens; he considers the evidence; then he and he alone makes the decisions.

In the Old Testament, the prophets did most of the intercessory praying. There were occasions when people prayed for themselves, but if something important was at stake, the people requested intercessory prayer, and the prophets took this responsibility seriously. First Samuel 12:23, speaking of the Israelites, says, "Far be it from me that I should sin against the Lord by ending my prayers for you."

Jeremiah was also a great intercessor for the people of Israel. He warned against false prophets, but he also said that if they were true prophets, they would have the word of the Lord in them, and they should also intercede for the people (Jer. 27:18).

Christ's death on the cross as the ultimate sacrifice has taken away the necessity for an intermediary here on earth. Now we can go directly to the Father with our prayers, because Christ is there at his right hand as our intercessor. And when we pray for others, we are the intercessors here.

Charles Whiston, in his book *Pray: A Study of Distinctive Christian Praying,* calls intercessory prayer a "spiritual blood donation." "Intercession is the giving of self to Christ, the giving of life, love, and energy to enter the lives of others through him for their blessing. We give to them not directly but through Jesus Christ. Direct giving might often be harmful, but intercession through Jesus Christ always benefits the other."

Very few people have the gift of tact. There is no foolproof way to point out someone's error without hurting him. Our tongues, more than any other thing, get us into trouble. A friend told me that when someone says to her, "I want to tell you this for your benefit because I love you," she immediately runs the other way. Inevitably, she is in for a reprimand, sometimes undeserved.

But we can and should pray for the person. And through prayer, we will come to understand the other's motives and not be so judgmatic. When we pray for someone, we don't need to tell God how to handle the problem. Often people say, "I don't know how to pray about this." In other words, they don't know what to tell the Lord to do about the problem. In such a case, don't be specific. The Lord knows that person's need. Just hold that person up to the Lord in holy intercession; let him decide what to do.

There are times when we should be specific and pray in faith for a definite solution. But if there are several options; if we feel uneasy about being specific; if we don't know which answer would be best, then we should simply intercede for that person. There is a great deal of difference between asking God for something and telling him what to do.

Paul spoke of this kind of prayer more than anyone else in the New Testament. Again and again in his epistles he asked for prayer for himself, and also stated that he was always praying for others.

The great aspect of this ministry of the interior is that anyone can do it. An invalid who cannot help others in any physical way or serve in a church can have an effective ministry by praying for others. The familiar expression, "if all else fails, read the instructions," applies to prayer. Prayer brings more results than ten new Sunday school programs and fourteen church suppers.

God actually gives some people a ministry of intercessory prayer. Suddenly they will feel compelled to pray. They describe it as an oppressive feeling, a heavy burden. They have no choice but to pray, right then, and often it will be a great deal later before they find out who they were praying for. They simply intercede in obedience to a definite inner calling to do so.

One such incident was related by Major Rupert Hazen, in *The Arizona Republic,* June 4, 1977, issue. He is now a U.S. Army chaplain stationed at Ft. Huachuca, Arizona.

During World War II, he was captured and interned in a German prison camp. He almost died there.

In his words: "I was incredibly weak, dying with fever and disease. A day before the camp was liberated by General George Patton's forces, the fever just left me and suddenly I was well. I was weak, but I was well."

Later, when he returned home to the little church where he had been converted, he learned that the minister's sister—whom he had never met—had heard a voice asking her to pray for Rupert Hazen, one day while she was hanging out the wash. She hadn't heard his name before.

"She said she would, but first wanted to finish the wash," he said. "The voice asked again, insisting that it be now." So she did pray, right there on the back steps.

"We checked the calendar and the international date line and found that this was the precise moment at which the fever left me," he said. "We sat down and cried."

There are certain ground rules for praying for others, and the most important one is our attitude. As was shown in the story of the missionary and the priest, without love our intercessory prayers are useless. They aren't on the right wave length; they aren't sincere.

This doesn't mean we have to genuinely love someone before we can pray for them; many times we pray for people we have never seen, and we know only their need of prayer. What it does mean is that we cannot harbor negative thoughts about the person we are praying for. Our prayer must be genuine.

A friend told me about an article in *Guideposts* that speaks of "creative-love praying." If we believe that God loves each of us perfectly and desires to meet our every need in his abundant way, we can pray for all of his blessing and joy for anyone we choose. Then as we pray, we can have perfect confidence that he hears and will answer, as he promised in I John 5:14-15.

So we simply see in our mind's eye all the qualities and benefits of God's love which we desire for our loved ones, friends, neighbors, and enemies as being realities in their lives through God's will and our prayers on their behalf. If we have faith that God is working and answering our prayers, we will not be discouraged if progress seems slow, but will thank God (by faith) that he is working. That means *we* don't have to carry the burden of setting people straight!

In Catherine Marshall's book, *Something More,* she relates the story of Clem and his sister Gladys. Gladys had prayed for Clem for twenty years. But he had not yet become a Christian, and his life was actually deteriorating. Twenty years of praying with no result! Then someone told her just to praise God for Clem, exactly the way he was. And so Gladys' prayers changed. She no longer pleaded with God (all the while harboring a condemning attitude toward Clem). She thanked God for him; praise had freed her from the position of judge.

Within five months from the time she began praying in this new way, Clem asked Jesus Christ to come into his life. There was an immediate radical change in him—all because of creative-love praying.

Negative thoughts act as a barrier which deflects prayers, just as a shield will deflect the sun's rays back into the atmosphere. Some of the rays get around the shield and reach the earth, but the strength of the sun's warmth is greatly diminished.

Picture an arena, a circle. Call this arena a circle of love. Every time we pray, we enter the circle of love. We come into the Divine Presence and enter the strongest force field in existence. When we pray for someone else, we take that person into the love circle with us. We expose him to the warmth of God's love.

If that person being prayed for is completely closed to the exposure—if he has his back turned to any positive spiritual force, he probably will not experience any benefit from the prayers. But I believe if enough people bring him into the circle of love often enough, eventually there will be a "thawing out." Bit by bit, the forces of love will break chinks in his armor and he will begin to respond to God.

Jesus gave us an example of intercessory prayer when he prayed for the disciples shortly before he was arrested. The entire prayer can be read in John 17:6-26. This prayer brims over with Christ's love for his followers. He was greatly concerned about them, about how they would fare after he was gone. He could have prayed this prayer silently or when he was alone. But he must have known that the words would bring comfort to the disciples after he was taken from them. He wanted to assure them they were not abandoned, but that he had placed them under the Father's protection.

The key to intercessory prayer is genuineness; we must have a very real concern for the person we are praying for, or the words will be hollow, meaningless.

There is no magic in numbers. When the fifty-second person prays for something, it isn't as if a Bingo light goes off in heaven announcing that we have hit the jackpot. Quality counts, as well as quantity. Two people who sincerely and earnestly pray about something upon which they are in agreement are more successful than hundreds who are not deeply concerned. Jesus said, "If two of you on earth agree in asking for anything it will be granted to you by my Heavenly Father" (Matt. 18:19). From this we deduce that if we have a large group praying for one single event, there will be more power. There *will* be—if the larger group is just as concerned as the two, or even the one. If all the pre-conditions are met by this larger group: if their own spiritual lives are clear; if they are not harboring negative thoughts, doubts, or misgivings about the request—then there will be more power. But a hundred people just mouthing the words of a prayer mean nothing.

One of the problems encountered with intercessory prayer is the guilt we feel when we forget to pray about something or someone. The more involved we become in the Christian life, the more people there are who will ask us to pray for them. It can actually get to the point that it becomes a burden.

One way to deal with this is not to include intercessory prayer in our daily prayer time. Leave this kind of praying for the rest of the day, to be done at any time, any place, whenever that person comes to mind. Often I have finished praying and then suddenly remembered someone and his request. Immediately I feel guilty and hastily add a P.S. But this isn't necessary; Paul says for us to pray without ceasing. We have all day, all night, for intercessory prayer. Every time that person comes to mind, breathe a short prayer for him; hold him up to the Father in holy intercession.

This method of intercessory prayer has a double benefit. When our regular prayer time is free from the list of petitions, we can spend much more time in confession, in just talking to the Father, and, hopefully, in praise and thanksgiving. It relieves the pressure of time limitation.

Leaving intercessory prayer out of my daily devotional time has done more than any other thing to improve the quality of my communion with the Father. This is not an unbreakable rule, of course. If something or someone is really pressing on my mind, I talk it over with the Father then and there. But that is different from going down my "list" of those I want to pray for. It frees me to relax and just come into his presence. I find myself doing much more soul searching now; I find much more to confess.

Hope MacDonald, in her book *Discovering How to Pray,* speaks of what she calls "arrow prayers." These are the little prayers which we shoot up to heaven all day long. Sometimes they are intercessory; sometimes they are for ourselves; but intercessory praying works well in the category of arrow prayers.

Another vital use of intercessory prayer is for our nation, for our President, for world peace. Often these areas seem so complex, so all-inclusive, that we tend to feel our tiny prayers would be useless. But what could possibly be more important? If we earnestly believe that prayer changes things, then we must pray for nations and international affairs. First Timothy 2:1 reads, "First, supplications, prayers, intercessions and thanksgiving should be made on behalf of all men: for kings and rulers in positions of responsibility, so that our common life may be lived in peace and quiet, with a proper sense of God and our responsibility to him for what we do with our lives. In the sight of God our savior this is undoubtedly the right way to pray; for his purpose is that all men should be saved and come to know that truth."

How often do we remember to include the President of our country in our intercessory prayers? Is this why we have so many wars, so much conflict—because we fail to pray? This verse in Timothy says to me that we have not, because we ask not. We throw out general prayers for peace now and then, especially in our church services. But wouldn't it be exciting to see what would happen if Christians all over the world banded together in common agreement to pray daily for world leaders?

There is a group called Intercessors for America who fast and pray on the first Friday of every month for our nation. Second Chronicles 7:14 gives a meaningful promise from God: "Then if my people will humble themselves and pray, and search for me, and turn from their wicked ways, I will hear them from heaven and forgive their sins and heal their land."

One absolutely essential principle of intercessory prayer is that of confidentiality. The trap of what I call Christian gossip is one which is so easy to fall into, especially for women.

We see someone in the grocery store and ask, "Have you heard how Kathy is getting along?"

"Fine, I guess—why, is something wrong?"

"Oh, I thought you knew. Oh, you must pray for her. . . ." And on we go to spill the whole story, all under the guise of "sharing."

The only person who has the right to share is the one who is experiencing the need. When a prayer request is made, it should be a solemn trust between two parties and it should go no further. Never assume that someone else already knows about the problem. The possibility of destroying a person's willingness to share his troubles in the future is so great that sometimes the damage is never undone. Some people close up and cut themselves off forever from the benefits of having others pray for them.

On the basis of scripture, prayers for healing must be almost always intercessory, rather than for ourselves. Paul was unable to pray successfully for the cure of his thorn in the flesh (whatever it was). Timothy could not pray for the healing of his stomach. And Christ did not pray for the cross to become lighter, for his wounds to be healed, or for his thirst to be quenched. Yet he could not stand to see others suffer.

Ethel, my neighbor and friend, had had a very serious operation. It was two days later, and she was not in pain, so she hadn't received any medication. [She checked this later to be sure she wasn't experiencing a euphoria from drugs.] As she lay in the hospital room, she began to feel a wonderful warmth surrounding her. She felt very peaceful and secure, as if she were an infant, wrapped in a pink woolen blanket. The feeling lasted for several hours.

The next day when her priest came to visit, she told him of her experience. "What time was this?" he asked. When she told him, he began to smile, "That was the exact hour our prayer group was praying for you!" The intercessory prayers were so full of love that she actually felt them there in her hospital room!

Prayer is tapping into the circle of love, the warmth of positive energy, the Son's rays!

Chapter VII

A Grain of Mustard Seed

A man came and knelt in front of Jesus. "Lord, have pity on my son," he said, "for he is a lunatic and suffers terribly. He is always falling into the fire or into the water. I did bring him to your disciples but they couldn't cure him."

"You really are an unbelieving and difficult people," Jesus returned. "How long must I be with you, and how long must I put up with you? Bring him here to me!"

Then Jesus spoke sternly to the evil spirit and it went out of the boy, who was cured from that moment.

Afterwards the disciples approached Jesus privately and asked, "Why weren't we able to get rid of it?" "Because you have so little faith," replied Jesus. "I assure you that if you have faith the size of a mustard-seed you can say to this hill, 'Up you get and move over there!' and it will move—you will find nothing is impossible." (Matt. 17:15-21)

Nothing is impossible—what a promise! Jesus wasn't disgusted with the man who brought his son to him; he was upset because the disciples could not cure the child. The disciples had been healing others with success, or the man would not have come to them. Yet this seemed too difficult—they didn't think they could handle it. After all he had taught them, after all they had seen him do, they still did not have enough faith.

This is another blockage of God's power; this is one more reason for unanswered prayer. Lack of faith is an elusive thing, easily overlooked and, if noticed, easily rationalized. We condemn ourselves least for this reason when our prayers are unanswered.

What is faith? How do we find it? How do we know if we have enough?

Whenever the word "faith" is used in the Bible, it is the Greek word which means to believe. It is translated "faith" in some instances and "belief" in others.

Faith is not desire. Faith isn't wanting something so much we will do anything to get it. God doesn't say, "according to how much you want it, so be it." He says, "according to your faith." Faith in what? Faith in him.

Often I think of faith as something I have to conjure up. Saying I have faith is like being on a fast-moving roller coaster with my eyes squeezed shut and fists clenched tightly on the bar, saying, "Isn't this fun!" when all the time I'm scared out of my wits. We say we have faith when we don't. We often misuse the word. "Oh, ye of little faith" has become a flippant remark, rather than an accusation, as it was originally.

In studying the scriptures in relation to faith in prayer, it would seem that our faith definitely affects whether or not our prayers are answered.

When Jesus came back to his own town of Nazareth, Matthew tells us he performed very few miracles there because of the people's lack of faith (Matt. 13:58).

Wouldn't you think that Jesus could have surmounted this unbelief and really put on a show for the hometown folk? Don't you imagine he was more hurt by their unbelief than that of anyone else and would

84

have loved to show them his complete splendor and power? Yet he wouldn't. He wouldn't transcend the laws of the universe which he himself set up. The negative thoughts and words uttered by the people of the town of Nazareth held back his power.

In the book of James we are told: "For the man who doubts is like a wave of the sea, carried forward by the wind one moment and driven back the next. That sort of man cannot hope to receive anything from the Lord, and the life of a man of divided loyalty will reveal instability at every turn" (James 1:6-8). This is clear—doubt is a huge deterrent. It is like a dam, keeping the full force of the water from flowing down the stream; it holds back the power.

Prayers of faith can be for wondrous miracles or for small, mundane needs, but either way, they are exciting. They give us a spiritual "high" because we know we are in touch with the Father.

A book replete with prayers of faith is *Realities*, by Mother M. Basilea Schlink of the Lutheran Sisterhood of Mary. This group of nuns in Germany lives by faith, and daily they experience the joy of being completely dependent upon their Father to provide for them.

Some years ago, they discontinued buying their food and personal needs. Money donated to the order is spent on equipment, building materials, and such. Their meals come from their garden as well as from donations of actual food. They do not even buy such things as toothpaste, soap, or other small personal items. They simply pray for what they need, and their Father always sends it to them. They derive such joy from receiving things in this manner—in Mother Basilea's words, "It is a greeting from the Father in heaven; it lets us know that He is thinking about us, that He has taken note of our needs; that He hears our prayers."

Reading story after story of their faith and its results, one is impressed with the fact that although they pray and do expect the answer to come, they still work diligently; they don't sit around waiting for the Father to feed them. They do manual labor of the type you would expect only men to do; they mix cement, build barns, drive heavy equipment, run printing presses—on and on goes the list.

They derive their fruits and vegetables from their garden; yet they ask for other things which they cannot grow, and they are always provided. One sister who works in the kitchen prayed for spices. Some of the others felt that was too extravagant; they thought spices were not a necessity and it was wrong to ask for them. But soon a box full of spices arrived as a gift, and they have never been without them since!

The principle here is a combination of faith and works. The Father does feed the sparrows and dress the lilies of the field. But sparrows and lilies do not have the brains and knowledge that we have. Although he wants us to be dependent upon him, especially for material things, that doesn't mean we should waste away our lives when they could be put to good use. Someone has to till the fields, spin the cloth, take care of the sick, and bake the bread. The world doesn't run on welfare. It is in forgetting to thank the Father for what he has given us—our jobs, our houses, our food; it is in taking credit ourselves for what we have, that we err.

There are times when we are given a special dose of faith to deal with the matter at hand. The earliest incidence of this in my life happened after our oldest daughter, Susan, had her tenth birthday.

She asked for a puppy, a dog of her very own. Our animals had always belonged to the entire family, but she wanted a pet which would be exclusively hers.

We found Josh through an ad in the paper. He was a cockerpoo, a mixture of cocker spaniel and poodle. He was only six weeks old, a tiny bundle of jet black hair, smooth as silk. As he grew, his hair lost its silky look and became shaggy, like that of an untrimmed poodle. Long strands began to droop down over his face, until soon you had to hunt to find his eyes. He and Susan were inseparable; she carried him around in her arms, and he slept on her bed.

Then one morning he disappeared. A quick look in the back yard revealed a hole dug under the fence. The entire family searched the neighborhood. Susan and her friend, Ann, knocked on doors, asking if anyone had seen a small, black dog.

But night came and no Josh. The next day, I called the radio station which advertises lost pets, and also put an ad in the newspaper. All that day, Susan circled the neighborhood, going even farther from home this time, but still there was no sign of him.

Toward evening of the second day, she really had given up. He was so very small; he could have been run over so easily. She loved him so much, she said through her tears; why did this have to happen?

As I held her, trying to comfort her, I suddenly knew—*knew*—that Josh would be found. I had told Susan all along we must pray about this. But now I told her God would answer her prayers and that Josh was going to come back. Going even further, I told her he would come back the next day!

After I had said these things, I realized what a risk I was taking. Having faith yourself is one thing, but telling a child that an event is going to happen is a little frightening. What if Josh didn't come back? What if I were wrong? How much damage would I have done to this child's faith?

The morning of the third day came. Nothing happened. The ad had appeared in the newspaper that morning, but we had no calls. Susan had given up her house-to-house canvass and tried to keep her mind off Josh. The day wore on, and I began to worry. I had said it would be today, hadn't I? And now the day was almost over. I busied myself in the kitchen, but I was afraid supper would be a cheerless meal.

Then the phone rang. It was a man who lived only two blocks away, on one of those funny cul-de-sacs which are so easy to pass by—one of the few areas Susan hadn't covered. He asked me some questions to make sure we were describing the same dog; then he told me Josh had been there all along, right from the first morning! The man had gone out to get his paper and Josh was sitting there, staring up at him with a whimsical look.

I cannot explain how I knew Josh was coming back; I only know that I did. There are times when the Father tells us things very clearly, and at those times, he wants us to tell others. The message and the answered prayer are supernatural; the stepping out in faith by telling others that the prayer will be answered is in the natural realm—that's our part.

In reading the stories which speak of Jesus' healing power, we notice that time after time Jesus said to the person, "Your faith has cured you," "Your faith has made you well," or "All things are possible to those who believe." When we read these comments, we get the impression that the person who is being prayed for must have faith, also.

But there are other accounts of Jesus' healings when there is no mention made of the person's faith. But notice when you read these accounts—there is no mention of doubt, either. In some cases, the people were simply bystanders—Jesus saw them, and felt such compassion that he healed them without a request from them. Or perhaps their requests were omitted from the written accounts of the incidents. Either way, the important thing to understand is that there was no doubt present.

When he said he would heal them, they didn't back away and say, "Now wait a minute, I don't want any faith healer fooling around with me!" They were willing to give him a chance; they were at least open to him. There was no negative energy blocking his power. Unanswered prayer, whether for healing or anything else, can probably be traced to lack of belief, more than any other reason.

What the Father loves to see in us is the kind of faith little children have. A friend of mine has a young daughter who, in the words of her mother, has a "hotline to heaven."

One story about Patricia I particularly like involved her brother's Little League game. The forecast was for rain that day; and sure enough, around two o'clock, the sky darkened and the clouds were a gray quilted blanket obscuring the sun. When her mother remarked that the game would probably be called off, Patricia said, "Don't worry, I've talked to God about it. It's going to be all right!"

Soon it began to rain, but because of Patricia's insistence that the game would be played on schedule, supper was served early, and Chris put on his uniform. As they left the house, the rain was still coming down.

When they approached the school, however, they could see it was not raining there—in fact, the field was perfectly dry. Patricia assured everyone who would listen that she had "talked to God about it" and it wasn't going to rain. The game proceeded, with thunder and lightning in the distance the entire time.

Just as the last out was called, and the players were coming off the field, the raindrops began to fall. Running for the shelter of their car, Patricia said, "See, I told you I talked to God about it!"

Most of us would identify with Peter, the apostle, more than with Patricia. He is my favorite disciple; he was always saying the wrong thing at the wrong time and seemed so utterly "human." I especially like the story of his attempt to walk on water.

Imagine being in that boat with the disciples. It is frightening to be out in the middle of a lake in a storm; it can be a very helpless feeling. I'm sure they had no lifejackets in those days, and if the boat were to capsize, one might as well have been on the ocean as far as the proximity of the shore was concerned.

The waves were becoming stronger and higher as the disciples frantically bailed water out of the boat. Where was Jesus? Why hadn't he come with them; maybe he could have helped! But Jesus didn't come. And the storm grew in intensity.

Not until the small hours of the morning did Jesus decide to walk out to where they were. He didn't do this just for show; there was no boat at the shore and it was the only way he could reach the others.

When the disciples saw a figure approaching, upright, actually walking—not on a lake which was smooth as glass, but through and over huge wind-whipped waves—they were frightened; they thought it must be a ghost. When Jesus saw their terror, he shouted to reassure them, "It's all right! It's I myself, don't be afraid!"

Peter instantly understood what Jesus was doing. He realized that Jesus had complete control over the elements of the universe, and he reasoned that if this were so, Jesus could give him that same power.

89

"Lord, if it's really you," he said, "tell me to come to you on the water."

"Come on, then," replied Jesus.

The account in Matthew goes on to say that Peter stepped down from the boat and did walk on the water toward Jesus. But when he felt the fury of the storm, he panicked and began to sink, calling out, "Lord, save me!" At once Jesus reached out and caught him, saying, "You of little faith! What made you lose your nerve like that?" Then, when they were both aboard the boat, the wind dropped. The whole crew came and knelt down before Jesus, crying, "You are indeed the Son of God!" (Matt. 14:25-33).

This story is a perfect example of the combination of faith and action. Peter did have faith that he could walk on the water if Jesus would give him that power. He asked for the power (in faith, believing). The power given to him by Jesus was supernatural—that came from God. But Jesus didn't lift Peter up out of the boat and place him on the water; that was completely natural. Peter got out of the boat of his own accord; he had to be willing to put first one foot, and then the other, onto the water. That took a lot of courage. But he looked steadily at Jesus, rather than looking down at the water, and he did it! He was actually walking toward Jesus on top of the water! Can you imagine how it thrilled Jesus to see him do that? At last, someone fully believed him, believed him to the point of overcoming the natural law of physics. Someone else was tasting the power which comes from being in touch with the Father.

But then something happened. Peter took his eyes off Jesus for a moment; he saw how fierce the waves were becoming and he panicked; he began to sink.

After Jesus pulled Peter up and they reached the boat, he asked him fondly, "What made you lose your nerve like that? Don't you have enough faith yet?"

Peter didn't answer. He was wet and cold and, most of all, disappointed in himself. But he shouldn't have been. At least he had tried; at least he had stepped out of the boat—that was more than the others had been willing to do. He had enough faith to step out, and there is the lesson for us. We must not only believe—we must *act* on that belief.

Faith is the epitome of positive energy. Doubt is negative, by its very definition. The minute Peter doubted, the supernatural power left—he lost it.

Acting on our belief is the difficult thing to do. It separates faith from "making believe."

My friend Jan Smith had no choice but to rely on the Father in a recent experience, and her "stepping out" was as frightening as Peter's adventure on the water.

Jan, her husband, Al, and their two children were in Zaire and had to go to Kenya for a training conference. The only way to get there was to drive through Uganda. It was August, 1976, just a few weeks after the Israeli raid on Entebbe, when the captives were freed so dramatically.

Tension was high. People in Zaire were of one opinion—that anyone traveling through Uganda at that time was asking for certain death. No gasoline was available there, and they were told that trying to carry enough for the trip was impossible, because it would be confiscated at the border.

After two weeks of prayer, Al announced that God had given him peace about this route, and Jan concurred. So in spite of all protests, they packed themselves, the suitcases, and two cans of gasoline into their Volkswagen and started out.

They bathed themselves in prayer. When they reached the Ugandan border they were asked to take everything out for inspection. Suitcases were looked into, the car was searched (this is standard procedure), and one of the guards asked what was in the jerry cans. "Gasoline," replied Al. "Okay, put everything back in and pass on through," was the casual reply.

They drove for eight hours across Uganda and marveled that they didn't see a single roadblock. These are routine even when the country isn't in a turmoil. Arriving in Kampala, the capitol city of Uganda, they stayed with some African friends who joyfully informed them why they had not been detained. It seems the Ugandan president had announced that morning that because his soldiers were exhausted from the past weeks of turmoil and killing, he was declaring a holiday for the troops.

The next day they drove on into Kenya without one single incident at border crossings. Their gasoline lasted just to the first gas pump inside Kenya, where their tank registered almost empty.

Jan wrote that they really hadn't expected the Lord to go that far just to ensure them a safe journey! She also warned that they don't recommend this type of action without specific guidance from the Lord.

Jesus prayed before raising Lazarus from the dead. He didn't go ahead rashly; he waited for guidance from the Father. Peter asked the Lord if he could come to him on the water. The answer came immediately, but Peter waited for the answer; he didn't step out without it.

Does all this sound far beyond your capabilities? Are you thinking that you could never pray with this kind of faith?

In Hebrews 11:11 we are told that faith means putting our full confidence in the things we hope for; it means being certain of things we cannot see. Many writers about the subject of prayer have attested to the value of visualizing the desired result as an aid to faith.

For instance, if a child is getting into trouble, doing badly in school, or whatever, picture that child in your mind as you want him to be. See him in your imagination as smiling, healthy, happy, doing well in school—whatever you desire for him.

This gives you a positive outlook; it keeps you from thinking the worst of that child every time anything wrong happens; it gives you confidence in him. It isn't just a game of pretend; it is the epitome of faith. What better understanding can there be of the verse from Hebrews than this—visualizing things as you want them to be—the evidence of things not seen.

Suppose you were able to foresee the future and you could see that child as an adult. As a man he is successful, happy, walking in a close relationship with the Lord, everything you could want for him. Armed with that knowledge, would the temporary phases that child is now going through upset you as much? Of course not; you would know the outcome; you would have confidence that he is going to turn out all right.

That is what God is saying to us here in Hebrews. The evidence of things not seen is the definition of faith. We pray in faith, take action on that faith (for example, do everything possible to see that the child has love and acceptance at home), and then have the patience to wait for the results.

Without faith, we produce negative results. If we think the worst of a person, he will not disappoint us; he will live up to our expectations, and this is especially true of children. None of us wants this for our children, of course, so we must believe in them, have faith in them.

But remember, there is a delicate balance between desire and faith. Picturing our daughters as the wives of millionaires and our sons as famous lawyers will probably lead to frustration and disappointment. There is a difference between imposing our wills on others' lives and praying for them in faith. One produces a negative relationship, while the other brings love and confidence into their lives, as well as ours.

Jesus told us, "Whatever you pray about and ask for, believe that you have received it and it will be yours" (Mark 11:24). This is the final act of the prayer of faith—to believe that we have received it.

One of the wisest men I know is Surrendra Gangadean, a philosophy professor at a local junior college. He was raised in the Hindu faith but was converted to Christianity while a university student. No matter what course he teaches, he quietly preaches the gospel along with it. The students respect him for his intellect, and therefore will listen to him when he speaks of Christ.

In explaining the concept of faith, he walks over to one of the students in the class with a set of car keys in his hand. He explains to the student that he is giving him a brand new car. There are the keys—all the student has to do is pick them up and the car is his. But as long as the student doesn't believe him the car will do him no good. It doesn't matter how often Mr. Gangadean tells him the car is his, the student must take the keys himself, or he will never get the new car.

So it is with prayer. Praying in faith takes three things. It takes confidence in the One to whom we are praying—God—confidence not only that he is *able* to do what we ask, but also that he *will* do what we ask. Of course, he will not do anything which is evil or harmful, no matter how much faith we have. But he delights in doing all sorts of little things for us, if only to prove he loves us. Psalm 37:4 reads, "Be delighted with the Lord. Then he will give you all your heart's desires."

Second, it takes enough faith to step out in that belief as Peter did, as Jan and Al Smith did, as little Patricia did.

And third, it takes the ability to hear the Holy Spirit when we are being told to pray for something. How do we hear? By practice. Each time we feel that inner nudge to go ahead and do something, and every time we obey, we are stepping up one more rung of the ladder toward learning to hear. We learn to hear by listening. We develop confidence in the ice by testing it; soon we can skate with confidence. So it is with prayer. The more our prayers of faith are answered, the more we will step out. Our mustard seed will grow and grow, until soon it is beautiful and in full bloom!

Chapter VIII

P.S. "If It Be Thy Will"

The scene is the home of Peter. The disciples and Jesus had been invited to dinner, but when they arrived, they were told by Peter's wife that her mother was very ill—she had a high fever. Jesus went in to see her. He laid his hand on her forehead, closed his eyes, and began to pray, "Father, please heal this woman if it is your will." Going back to the others, he told them he had prayed for her healing, but they would have to wait and see what happened.

She grew worse. They not only had to fix their own dinner, they also had to care for her.

Is that the way the story is told in the New Testament? Or does it really go like this: "Then, on coming into Peter's house Jesus saw that Peter's mother-in-law had been put to bed with a high fever. He touched her hand and the fever left her. And then she got up and began to see to his needs" (Matt. 8:14, 15).

Jesus knew it was his Father's will to heal her; he didn't need to ask.

He didn't put a lid on his or the woman's faith by the addition of the words "if it be thy will."

So often our prayers go like this: "Oh, Lord, please heal my Aunt Susie in Minneapolis, if it be thy will." Or we close our prayers with the statement, "and we commend all these things to you, Father, if it be thy will." And so the weekly prayer meeting goes, or should we say the "weakly" prayer meeting. The people hastily add their little insurance policy onto the end of each prayer.

Who is the beneficiary of this insurance policy? Is it God? Are we protecting him? Or is it ourselves; are we protecting ourselves from losing faith if the prayer isn't answered?

I believe it is both. We don't want God to lose face, and we somehow think it is up to us to save him from embarrassment. If one stops to think about it, this is really the height of arrogance; we don't need to protect God's reputation. If we do not believe he is able and willing to answer a prayer we put forth, then we had better reexamine our request. But in addition to trying to save God from humiliation, we are saving ourselves. If we pray in faith, believing, and the prayer isn't answered, we have been put in a vulnerable position. We don't want to be hurt—either by God or by others who have heard the prayer.

This little phrase, "if it be thy will," is a hangup which bothers many people. Before our group studied this, we were under the impression that it was a biblical method of prayer. We vaguely remembered phrases which spoke of "God's will." But how much was actual scripture and how much was tradition came as a surprise. Also, studying each verse in which God's will was mentioned in context shed much light on the problem.

Paul frequently used the term "God's will" in his letters to the young churches. But he was never speaking in reference to prayer. He said such things as, "I hope to spend some time with you, if it is the Lord's will" (I Cor. 16:7), but you can be sure he sought God's will through prayer first. Do you see the difference? He would ask God for guidance, ask him to show him where he was to go next on his journeys. Paul was head honcho on the missionary circuit; he wasn't just friend-hopping around the country. He went only where God told him to go; he went only where he was needed.

The one who first framed this phrase was James, who wrote the practical handbook for Christian living. He tells us:

> Just a moment, now, you who say, "We are going to such-and-such a city today or tomorrow. We shall stay there a year doing business and make a profit!" How do you know what will happen tomorrow? What, after all, is your life? It is like a puff of smoke visible for a little while and then dissolving into thin air. Your remarks should be prefaced with, "If it is the Lord's will, we shall still be alive and will do so-and-so." As it is, you take a certain pride in planning with such confidence. That sort of pride is all wrong. (James 4:13-16)

Notice there is no mention here of prayer. He is talking about our attitude toward life. James is saying we must seek God's will (through prayer, since this is how we communicate with him), and then we will be able to pray in faith.

Probably the most familiar passages regarding the will of God are those which quote Jesus. In Matthew 6:10, which is part of the Lord's prayer, Jesus says these words, "Your will be done on earth as it is in Heaven." In the Greek, this is in the imperative tense, as if it were a command. In Matthew 26:39, Christ is praying in the Garden of Gethsemane: "He . . . fell on his face and prayed, 'My Father, if it be possible let this cup pass from me—yet it must not be what I want, but what you want.' " In John 4:34, when the disciples were worried because Jesus wasn't eating, he said, "My food is doing the will of him who sent me and finishing the work he has given me." Again, in the Gospel of John, Christ says: "By myself I can do nothing. As I hear from God, I judge, and my judgement is true because I do not live to please myself but to do the will of the Father who sent me" (John 5:30).

In none of these statements did Jesus say "if it is thy will"; he said "thy will be done." There is a great deal of difference between these two phrases.

"Thy will be done" means that God's intentions for this world be carried out (by us); that whatever he intends for us to do, whatever are his wishes for us, be allowed to happen. We are praying that we will not be the barrier which prevents God's supreme will from being done. We are relinquishing our will to his.

In the words of F. W. Woods in *Praying God's Way: Essays on Prayer:* "Prayer is not an attempt to overcome God's will but an endeavor to embrace his willingness. Prayer is not bringing our wishes to God to coax Him to make them His own; it is not an attempt to convert God to our way of thinking, but it is resigned, yielded, asking according to His will."

This isn't easy for us to do. It is hard to turn over our will, our free will, to the Father. And it isn't something we do only once. It is a constant turning over of our will in each situation.

How do we know God's will? There are countless scriptures which show clearly what his will for us is, and we can be certain that what he promises in his Word is according to his will. But what about the areas which are not specifically mentioned in scripture?

To quote from the anonymous author of the book *The Kneeling Christian:* "In the first place, we must not expect God to reveal His will to us unless we desire to know that will and intend to do that will. Knowledge of God's will and the performance of that will go together. We are apt to desire to know God's will so that we may decide whether we will obey or not. Such an attitude is disastrous. 'If any man will do His will, he shall know of the teaching' (John 7:17)."

In the great majority of cases, we already know God's will in a given situation. It may take us a long time to make a decision, and so we think of this as a lengthy period of time during which we did not know God's will. But in most cases, we do know which route God would prefer us to take; it is only our inner rebellion which gives us the excuse of making it a choice between two courses.

However, when there is a decision to be made between two seemingly equal choices, we should seek God's will through prayer. We should lay the problem out before the Father and then pray in faith for positive guidance toward the correct way. And we are not left alone in this prayer; the Holy Spirit will help us. "We do not know how to pray worthily, but his Spirit within us is actually praying for us in those agonizing longings which cannot find words. He who knows the heart's secrets understands the Spirit's intention as he prays according to God's will for those who love him" (Rom. 8:26).

Having asked for guidance, we must be willing to wait. The answer comes in different ways to different people and at different times. It may come directly as a thought or as a still, small voice. It may come from a closed opportunity, which signifies a negative answer; it may come through other people and circumstances. Often, people find guidance from a scripture passage which the Lord gives them, either one which they had not noticed before or a very familiar passage which suddenly acquires new meaning when applied to the present situation.

Some might offer the objection that there are times when the lines are drawn less clearly—when the situation is gray, rather than black and white. For instance, a person has a choice of two jobs and doesn't know which to take. Should he or she pray, "If it be thy will I will take this job over the other"? No, the person should go to God in earnest desire for his guidance and ask for definite leading. If the prayer is, "I want this job (if it is your will), rather than that other one," that is not seeking God's will at all; that is telling God what to do.

What if no answer comes? What if there is no objective (or subjective) leading toward either job? If the person knows that either job would not be *against* God's will, then he or she should simply step out in faith, and choose the one most desired. Sometimes we blame God for our indecisiveness; sometimes we use him as an excuse for our procrastinations. If we are living in his will in all other areas of our life and if no red light is put in front of us about a decision, then we should just go ahead and do it!

If God's will isn't clear in a certain matter, there is no way to pray in faith. Saying "if it be thy will" at the end of a prayer completely negates everything for which we have just prayed. It makes the prayer useless; it is like saying, "If you were going to do this anyway, Lord, it's okay with me. But if you weren't going to do it, never mind." If doubt is a power blockage which keeps a prayer from being answered, then these words are the method by which that doubt is expressed.

"And this is the confidence which we have in him, that if we ask anything according to his will he hears us. And if we know that he hears us in whatever we ask, we know that we have obtained the requests we made of him" (I John 5:14, 15 RSV). Even here, the "if" is a condition put upon us, not upon God. "If we ask anything according to his will"—there again, we should know his will before we ask—how else can we ask according to his will?

When Christ was praying in the garden, he knew the Father's will; he knew he must die on the cross. But in his humanness, he was asking if there was another way out. He said, "If it be possible, let this cup pass from me"—if there is any other way this can be accomplished. But there wasn't. And Christ was obedient; he did the Father's will.

If adding this phrase to our prayers were a valid way to pray, we would use it consistently, but we don't. We don't pray, "Please keep my children safe today, if it is your will." We say instead, "Please keep my children safe," and we feel very secure when we have done this because we have entrusted them to the Father's safekeeping. We know it is his will to keep them safe.

We don't ask the Father to bring someone into a relationship with him and add "if it is your will" because we know it is the Father's will for everyone to come to know him. A prayer like this may take years to be answered, but that is because the other person's will may be set against God's. Our wills are very often different from his, and he never interferes with the freedom he has given us.

We so often dismiss unanswered prayers as not being God's will; that is the easy way out. It is much harder to think through the various reasons in our own lives which might have prevented our prayers from being answered; it is much harder to admit that we ourselves might be the reason our requests were denied.

There are many variables in prayer, but if all blockages are removed—blockages of guilt, doubt, unforgiveness, insincerity, hate, and so on, and if we have sought God's will through a search of the scriptures, and through prayer, then we should never have to say "if it is thy will."

I belong to a Christian writers' group. We meet once a month to critique one another's work, share our problems, encourage and pray for one another. Jan Potter, one of the women in the group, wanted to attend a Christian writers' seminar. It was to be a week-long session, with writers and editors teaching and evaluating the students' work. But Jan's husband had some reservations as to whether the trip was necessary. She earnestly wanted to be in God's will in this matter, and she did not want to go if her husband wasn't entirely in agreement.

Jan shared these thoughts with us in our meeting. As we were leaving that day, I said, "Let's all promise to pray daily that Jan will be able to go to the seminar." One of the others warned, "Well, we better pray she can go if it's God's will." I immediately responded, "I'm going to write an entire chapter on that in my book about prayer—don't pray that way!"

I came home and did pray in faith that Jan could go to the conference. Two of the other women prayed "if it be thy will," and one of them told me later she really was afraid Jan was going to be terribly discouraged if she couldn't attend. She asked the Lord to help overcome the disappointment.

As it turned out, a series of events occurred which completely changed her husband's mind, and Jan not only went to the seminar, but became acquainted with one of the editors, who subsequently bought an article she had written. At that point in her life, she desperately needed some reassurance of her writing ability.

Four of us had prayed. But I had not added the "doubt clause." I had no doubt that it was the Lord's will for Jan to go to the conference. If I had been unsure, I could not have prayed in faith.

The psalmist says that God wants us to have the desires of our heart. Satan loves for us to add "if it be thy will" to a prayer because he knows it is a negative blockage to the power of God. It is doubt personified— the opposite of faith. God's will is whatever is best for us. We are the

101

ones who constantly put the brakes on him; we hold him back as he reaches out to bless us.

In reading the accounts of the disciples after they had been given power through prayer, you will notice that what they asked for was evidently in line with God's will. We don't read that Peter asked for a late-model chariot or Mary Magdalene asked for diamonds and pearls. We only see them asking for guidance for their infant church and its struggles; praying for those who were in prison, and, more than anything else, praying for the healing of others. They knew it was God's will to heal—they never doubted it. Yet it is in prayers for healing that we are most prone to tack on our pet phrase "if it be thy will."

I do not believe it is ever God's will for anyone to be ill. How can I say this? Because Jesus never looked at someone who was crippled, had leprosy, or was sick in any way and hesitated. He didn't say, "Well, maybe it would teach them patience to be sick a while longer. There is something I want them to learn through this."

God wants us to live abundantly. Jesus said, "I am come that they might have life, and that they might have it more abundantly" (John 10:10 KJV). He wants the very best imaginable life for us. He wants us to be free, to fulfill our potential as human beings, to look our best, and to be our best, both physically and emotionally. Then what is wrong? Why are there so many of us who are not in perfect health?

There are basically three reasons. First, there is an evil force in this world and from him proceed all imperfections. It is Satan's will that these things occur.

Then there are cause-and-effect realities. If there are germs loose on Planet Earth, some of us are going to be affected by those germs. If a child runs into the street, and if a driver is careless, it is likely that the child will be hit. If God were to interfere and stop the consequences of cause and effect in every instance, there would be no reason for personal responsibility. It is not God's will for a smoker to develop lung cancer; it is not his will that we kill one another in wars; it is not his will that there be birth defects.

An article in *Time,* June 13, 1977, issue, pointed out the extent to which we bring destruction upon ourselves. Under the "Environment" section, the article read:

> Some forms of cancer are caused by such natural factors as heredity and viruses. But many cancers are brought on—especially in the industrialized parts of the world—by environmental factors. As the U N report explains, the cancers "relate to the air people breathe or the water they drink, to the environment in which they work or live, to their personal diet or way of life." In industrialized societies, environmental factors have already been proved to be responsible for up to 40% of all human cancers; for example, doctors have found a high incidence of an otherwise rare form of lung cancer in workers exposed to asbestos, and are discovering another rare form of liver cancer among those who have worked with vinyl chloride. In 1958, a British physician named John Higginson was challenged by a skeptical scientific community when he suggested that 70% to 80% of all cancers are environmental in origin. Now many scientists suspect that the actual figure may be closer to 90%.

There is another and probably more prevalent reason for our lack of perfection—ourselves. We are usually our own worst enemies. We perpetrate all sorts of calamities upon ourselves by our self-destructive behavior. A good book to read along this line is *Prayer Can Change Your Life,* by William Parker and Elaine St. Johns. This fascinating book records scientific prayer "experiments" which took place over a ten-year period. In prayer groups, it was proven that blockages inside the people prevented them from receiving answers to prayer. God was there, ready to grant their wishes, but until they were able to release themselves from bondages such as fear, guilt, hate, and inferiority feelings, the symptoms of their illnesses persisted.

God's will is not always done here on earth. God is blamed for many things which aren't his will at all.

Recently the newspapers told of a lady in Indiana who was murdered. Over nine million dollars which she had stashed in various places in her house was stolen. The guilty persons were found, but the story related that there was no reason for them to have murdered their

103

victim. She had been robbed twice previously and each time she had refused to prosecute. Why? Because she said, "It was God's will for me to be robbed."

Oh, how we malign God! We praise him and say he is the author of all goodness and then actually believe he wills all sorts of terrible things for us.

Why *was* the woman robbed? Because she refused to trust banks; she stored her money herself. This is comparable to lying down on the railroad tracks and then saying it is God's will if you are run over. Why was she murdered? Because some people are totally egocentric, totally godless; they answer only to themselves. When they saw an opportunity to get a great deal of money, it didn't matter to them if they had to kill to get it. It was not God's will that they did this; it was *their* will, their will against God's. "Thou shalt not steal; thou shalt not kill."

We may be confused by the concept that God's will is for our best interests and the fact that he allows evil things to happen. Since we know God has complete control of the universe; since the battle between him and Satan is not evenly matched, but God is supreme, we think that if he doesn't intervene in a situation, then the result must be his will. But this isn't necessarily so. Just because he "allows" something to happen (that is, doesn't step in to prevent it) does not mean it is his will. To some extent, the reasons for evil in the world will remain a mystery as long as we are on earth. God's ultimate plan will be carried out. However, because our wills are very often against that of God, the course of history doesn't run smooth.

"If it be thy will" at the end of a prayer is like water dashed on the fire of faith; it is our way out, if the prayer isn't answered. It was never used that way in the scriptures.

One day a leper fell down before Jesus' feet. " 'Sir,' he said, 'if you want to, you can make me clean.' Jesus stretched out his hand and placed it on the leper saying, 'Of course I want to. Be clean!' " (Matt. 8:3).

"Of course I want to." But we must want to, too. Sometimes we pray negatively; sometimes we don't want an event to happen, but we resignedly pray "If this is what you want for me, Lord—I'll just have to accept it." This isn't just a game in semantics; it reflects an attitude. There is a wide gulf between giving *in* to God and giving *up* on God. Perhaps the chapter on the prayer of surrender will make this difference more clear.

Again quoting from the anonymous author of *The Kneeling Christian:* "When we lift up our souls to God in prayer it gives God an opportunity to do what He will in us and with us. God is always at our side, but we are not always at His side."

Prayer is the catalyst.

Chapter IX

The Prayer of Surrender

The last chapter contrasted the phrases "thy will be done" and "if it be thy will." But what is the difference between praying in faith and praying in surrender? Is the prayer of surrender just another way to say "if it be thy will"? Is the prayer of surrender the antithesis of the prayer of faith?

Again, we must categorize prayer. Each prayer must be taken on its own merit, framed in the circumstances of the moment and not lumped under the umbrella word "prayer."

The prayer of surrender is not a prayer to be used often; it is to be used only in certain circumstances, under the guidance of the Holy Spirit, and usually when all else has failed. It is the prayer to use when we have hit bottom, when our faith is weak, when our prayers seem to be hitting the ceiling and bouncing back, going nowhere and being heard by no one.

It is a prayer which is hard to describe, because it is difficult to learn, other than through experience. To read about it is interesting on a theoretical level, but true understanding comes only when it is used, when it becomes a reality in our own lives.

That understanding came to me when our daughter Susan faced a serious operation a few years ago. I'll never forget the events which preceded those hours of apprehension and fear.

Susan was then fourteen and had owned a horse for several years. She and a friend were leading their horses back to the stable when suddenly the friend's horse struck out, knocking Susan down. The wind was knocked out of her, but she got up in a moment, and when she came home she mentioned the incident only casually.

But toward bedtime she began complaining of pain. We took her to the emergency room for X-rays, thinking she might have some broken ribs, but the X-rays were negative.

The next day she stayed home from school, complaining that it hurt when she laughed. I gave her aspirin and told her to take it easy, but the next day when she again insisted she couldn't go to school, I took her to our doctor.

Phil is a friend, and the following week his family and ours were planning a skiing trip to Colorado. He examined Susan. "I may be overreacting," he said, "but since we're going skiing next week, I'd like you to take her to see a surgeon. There's a chance she could have a ruptured spleen."

After the surgeon examined Susan, he told me to put her in the hospital immediately for observation. We went directly to the hospital and within an hour, she was given a battery of X-rays. There it was—the oversized spleen. It had not shown up two days earlier because the hematoma had not yet developed.

Since they wanted to run some more tests, the surgery wasn't scheduled until the next day.

When I walked into the hospital room the next morning, I knew Susan's condition had deteriorated during the night. She was pale and lethargic, greeting me wanly.

I sat beside her, holding her hand, and we prayed together. Then she dozed for a while and I laid my head down on her bed, exhausted. Exhausted, frustrated, and scared.

Since the beginning of this ordeal, I had prayed continually. The night before, I had made a few hasty phone calls and asked for prayer from others. But nothing was doing any good, for me or for her. I wasn't receiving any peace, and my prayers were becoming rote, repetitious, hollow. I felt abandoned by God. I couldn't understand why he wasn't real to me right then, when I needed him most.

I was begging God to take care of Susan, imploring, pleading. Why couldn't I pray in faith? What had happened to all the prayer promises about asking and receiving? What was wrong with me? Nothing was happening! I was growing more frightened, and Susan was getting worse.

Then suddenly I remembered something I had read in Catherine Marshall's book, *Beyond Our Selves,* about the prayer of relinquishment. She told the story of Nathaniel Hawthorne's daughter, when she was gravely ill. The parents had been told she would probably not live through the night. The distraught mother had been battling with God, saying, "She must not, cannot die." Then, unexpectedly, the thought came into her mind that God is sovereign. If he wanted to take her daughter, it must be for the best. Only then did she experience peace. And only then did the child's fever break—she recovered!

All this flashed through my mind in an instant, and in the same way Sophia Hawthorne had intuitively known what she must do, so did I. The Holy Spirit gave me the clear knowledge that I must "give" Susan to God.

By this time she was asleep. I held her hand and laid my head on the bed beside her. Then I prayed a simple prayer of surrender. I thanked God for giving her to us. I told him how grateful I was to have had her for fourteen years; I told him what a joy she had been. And I gave her back to him, telling him since he had given her to us in the beginning, I had no right to hold on to her. I relinquished my will for her survival.

Immediately, a flood of peace came over me—it was like a release. I cannot adequately describe the difference in how I felt one moment—uptight, full of fear, nervous, and then in the next instant, the exact opposite—calm, peaceful, at rest. There was no assurance that Susan was going to be all right. God hadn't spoken to me to let me know the outcome of the surgery. But I had in essence said, "Thy will be done; you know what is best."

Previously I had been holding onto her, clutching her, and yet at the same time crying out to God for help. But he couldn't help, not until I released her to him. I never doubted it was his will to heal her. But as long as I was holding onto her, I was dictating to God, telling him what he *must* do. My prayers were negative, demanding, filled with apprehension.

Fear is the antithesis of trust. Fear is saying, "I don't trust you, God." But the prayer of surrender says, "Whatever you decide will be best—you are God."

After the operation, the surgeon and Phil talked to my husband and me. They said Susan was fine; everything went well. But the surgeon commented, "I can't understand it. That spleen was twice its normal size. It was just about ready to rupture—I don't know why it didn't!"

Then the most chilling statement of all came from Phil. He said, "You know, I didn't sleep very well last night. I kept thinking about what would have happened if we had been up on that ski slope and her spleen had ruptured."

"Oh," I immediately protested, "we wouldn't have made the trip with her in that much pain."

"You don't understand," he replied. "The symptoms can go away completely and then suddenly the spleen will burst!"

I fully realized then what a close call Susan had had. And my gratitude for her well-being overflowed.

Later that day, as I sat beside her, I realized the full meaning of the prayer of surrender. I began to understand that we don't have to wait for a crisis to turn things over to the Lord. There were several areas in my life which I needed to turn over to him then, and whatever happened in the future, I would know he was in control. I would no longer be clutching, maintaining my independence in those areas.

I realized there is no contradiction between the prayer of faith and the prayer of surrender. The prayer of faith is used when there is no fear, when we are trusting God in the area we are praying about, when we know what his will is, for that particular thing. But the prayer of surrender is for those times when we have tried all else and failed; when we are filled with doubt; when the way is dark.

The prayer of surrender comes into our lives when we are holding something back from God, whether it be a child or a habit or a sin. There is a principle of sacrifice here that is necessary for each of us to learn as we mature in our faith.

It was a principle which Abraham had to learn. The story of Abraham, as told in Genesis, is a fascinating account of a man who completely trusted God. Abraham was one hundred years old, and Sarah his wife was ninety-one; yet God promised them a son. When that day came, there was much rejoicing, because Isaac was truly a miracle child. He grew into a fine young man and was the delight of his parents.

But one day the Lord spoke to Abraham. We join the narrative as it is given in *The Living Bible:*

"Abraham!" God called.

"Yes, Lord?" he replied.

"Take with you your only son—yes, Isaac whom you love so much—and go to the land of Moriah and sacrifice him there as a burnt offering upon one of the mountains which I'll point out to you!"

The next morning Abraham got up early, chopped wood for a fire upon the altar, saddled his donkey, and took with him his son Isaac and two young men who were his servants, and started off to the place where God had told him to go. On the third day of the journey Abraham saw the place in the distance.

"Stay here with the donkey," Abraham told the young men, "and the lad and I will travel yonder and worship, and then come right back."

Abraham placed the wood for the burnt offering upon Isaac's shoulders, while he himself carried the knife and the flint for striking a fire. So the two of them went on together.

111

"Father," Isaac asked, "we have the wood and the flint to make the fire, but where is the lamb for the sacrifice?"

"God will see to it, my son," Abraham replied. And they went on.

When they arrived at the place where God had told Abraham to go, he built an altar and placed the wood in order, ready for the fire, and then tied Isaac and laid him on the altar over the wood. And Abraham took the knife and lifted it up to plunge it into his son, to slay him.

At that moment the Angel of God shouted to him from heaven, "Abraham! Abraham!"

"Yes, Lord!" he answered.

"Lay down the knife; don't hurt the lad in any way," the Angel said, "for I know that God is first in your life—you have not withheld even your beloved son from me."

Then Abraham noticed a ram caught by its horns in a bush. So he took the ram and sacrificed it, instead of his son, as a burnt offering on the altar." (Gen. 22:1-13)

In the New Testament, Abraham is called the friend of God because he, too, was called upon to sacrifice his son, just as the Father did.

But notice that Isaac was spared; it was only Abraham's willingness which God was asking for. The same truth applied to me when I was willing to give Susan to God.

There is a daily method of surrender to God through prayer which has caught my imagination. It is called the "Snowflake Prayer" and is related by Charles Whiston in his book *Pray: A Study of Distinctive Christian Praying.* The author makes the point that it requires far more than a single brief conversion experience to achieve the transfer of sovereignty from self to Christ. It involves a sustained, lifelong action. In his words:

A single snowflake, seen through a magnifying lens, is very beautiful in design. No two snowflakes are identical; each one has individuality. Each snowflake is so fragile that one has only to breathe upon it and it is destroyed. But during winter storms and blizzards God dumps billions of tiny, weak, fragile snowflakes upon the higher levels of the mountain ranges where they build up a massive snowpack 20 or 30 feet in depth. The snowpack settles under its accumulated weight and at the bottom is compressed and congealed into solid ice. Loose fragments of granite rock lying on the surface of the ground are frozen into this ice. As the snowpack inches down the mountain, these rock chips become the chisel edges that God uses to grind down solid masses of granite rock into fine granules of sand, which the melting snows in spring will carry down the mountainside to deposit in river and lake beds. Hard granite is broken down by weak snowflakes.

So, too, God erodes man's hardness of heart by repeated use of the Snowflake Prayer of surrender. Said once or used only occasionally, the prayer is impotent. But prayed daily over decades of life, such a prayer effects mighty changes in our lives.

He goes on to suggest that this be done every morning before getting out of bed, when we first wake up. He says we should picture Jesus standing by the bed and say to him, "I give myself again to you this day, all that I am, all that I have, to be unconditionally yours for your use. Take me away from myself and use me where you will, when you will, as you will, with whom you will."

This prayer said over and over again will have a deep subconscious effect, day after day after day, wearing down the granite of "self" in our hearts.

The prayer of faith and the prayer of surrender are two distinctly separate ways to pray, each to be used at the proper time. And yet, they are intertwined. Ideally, each of us would turn over his whole life, his whole self to God, and then the prayer of surrender would be nothing but an extension of that one act in time. But in reality, we don't do this. We turn over one area of our lives, and then usually, we snatch it back. Hopefully, as our lives progress, we will be able to turn over more and more to God and take back less and less. Then we could always pray in faith.

But prayers of faith can be used whether we are totally surrendered or not. Prayers of faith don't involve our wills; they only involve external things. I have prayed in faith that our high school team would win a track meet; I have prayed in faith that God would help me find something I have lost; I have prayed in faith for someone's healing.

But none of these things involved my will. My will wasn't set against God's. I wasn't demanding; I was simply asking, the way a child asks, in trust.

In the incident with Susan, my fear negated my faith. I wanted God to help, but there was so much negative energy rising from my distraught emotions that I wasn't able to pray effectively. I couldn't help my fear; it was a natural emotion at a time like that. But the only cure for that fear was to turn over my will to God.

The prayer of surrender is saying "Thy will be done." It is not saying, "Heal her, if it is thy will." It is God's will to heal, but he must have total possession first. We can't hold back, and expect him to accomplish a miracle.

If the Snowflake Prayer is said each day, we can always pray in faith, knowing that we have turned over everything in our lives to the Father's loving care.

Chapter X

The Prayer of Praise

Praise God from whom all blessings flow;
Praise God all creatures here below;
Praise Him above ye heavenly host;
Praise Father, Son, and Holy Ghost. Amen.

The well-known words of the Doxology are sung by many of us in our churches as the morning offering is brought to the altar. As with the Lord's Prayer, the words are so familiar we seldom listen to them; often they are sung heedlessly, praise being the last thing on our minds.

A study of prayer would not be complete without delving into the prayer of praise. If we never offered any other kind of prayer, praise would be sufficient; it is really the most important kind of prayer.

What is praise? How does it differ from thanksgiving? And why is it so important in our prayer life?

Praise is defined as an expression of approval or commendation, the glorifying and honoring of a god, ruler, hero, etc., especially worship of God expressed in song (Funk and Wagnall's Standard College Dictionary).

The psalms are praise expressed in song. Some of the most moving hymns are those of psalms which have been set to music. The purpose of music in a worship service is to praise God. But somehow as the church grew, it became more formal and dignified, and the concept of praise was left further and further behind. This was reflected in the music, as well as in the prayers. It is only recently as churches are experiencing renewal that a sense of joy has returned to some of our worship services.

But praise is not to be limited to a once-a-week happening. Praise can and should become a very real and ever-present part of our daily lives.

A study of the word "praise" throughout the scriptures shows it is used much more frequently in the Old Testament than in the New. In the New Testament, the word "thanksgiving" is more prevalent. I tried to find a slight differentiation of meaning between the two words, but in studying them in context, I came to the conclusion that they were interchangeable. We thank God for who he is, what he has done (not only for us, but for everyone), and in that "thanks giving," we are praising him.

As in any scriptural principle, it is the motive that counts. We all can tell the difference when someone is truly paying us a compliment, or going out of his way to show gratitude, and when we are given an empty, polite "thank you." Empty words of praise are as meaningless to the Father as are our polite generalities to one another.

It was in Catherine Marshall's book *Something More* that I first encountered the concept of praise as being a sacrifice to God. When we praise in the face of trouble, we are sacrificing our right to grumble. "Well, I have a perfect right to be mad," we say, or "Who wouldn't complain about all these calamities." Praise as a sacrifice is the giving up of our natural emotions, linking them to the Lord's power. Then he is able to lift us above the trouble and it is easier for us to cope with it.

Psalm 50:14 puts it this way: "What I want from you is your true thanks." And in Leviticus 19:24 we are told to give an offering of praise. Hebrews 13:15 puts it more succinctly with these words: "Let us offer a sacrifice of praise to God—the tribute of lips which openly acknowledge his name."

This concept makes it easier for me to praise when I don't feel like praising. Thinking of it as a sacrifice, I picture myself laying my "right" to complain upon an altar to God. It is a gift to him and one he appreciates very much. God "inhabits the praises of Israel," we are told in the Psalms. This means that when we praise, he is with us in that praise. Praise draws God to us and us to God.

There have been many books written in the past few years which tell us to praise God for everything, and cite story after story of lives and circumstances which have been changed because of this attitude of praise. But some just cannot accept this idea of praising God for evil events, and because of that, forego praise altogether, or praise God only for the good things which happen to them.

I feel there has been an error in interpretation. I do think we should praise God *in* every single circumstance of our lives. But I cannot go along with the thinking that we thank Him *for* the circumstance. Of all the verses in the Bible that speak of thanksgiving, there is only one that tells us to thank God *for* everything. All the rest say to thank God *in* everything.

For example, when a child is ill, we continue to thank God for everything he has done for us, for the child, for our own health, and everything else we can possibly think of, but we do not praise him *for* the illness. However, while praising him during and *in* the illness, the mystery of praise takes effect. We change; circumstances change; his power is unleashed.

We are not praising God for doing something evil to us or to the child. Instead, we are saying, "I'm not too happy about this, Lord, but I'm going to praise you in the midst of all this trouble. I'm not going to focus on the trouble, I'm going to focus on you. I'm going to reflect on your goodness and let your healing energy flood my soul so this trouble won't get me down."

When something bad happens, there are several ways we can react. We can panic, think of the very worst possible result, and spread our fear to others by loud and constant verbal worrying. This is a negative reaction.

Or we can suppress our fear, hold it in, smile, and remain calm. This is a neutral reaction. We don't harm others with this reaction; they may even admire us and speak later of what a peaceful spirit we have. But we do damage to ourselves. We push the fear and doubt and anger down deep inside, and it will eventually emerge as a physical or emotional illness.

The third alternative is to admit the problem, admit the fear (especially to God in prayer), and then to begin praising God, not for the trouble, but for all our other blessings.

It isn't that we are thanking God for our trouble; he didn't cause it. Most of the time it happened simply as a result of cause-and-effect reality, or Satan had a hand in it, or we ourselves are to blame. But Romans 8:28 tells us that God fits everything into a pattern for good to those who love God and are called according to his plan. In other words, he takes the illness or whatever trouble we are experiencing, and eventually turns it into something good for us.

Praise releases his power because it represents the epitome of positive energy. Fear and grumbling and griping block that power.

Going back to the analogy of prayer as a type of energy, a prayer of praise would be the very highest current possible. Praise immediately links us to God in a mysterious way. In Catherine Marshall's words, "Praise is the genius instant shortcut to the power of God."

Praise lifts the clouds of doubt and fear and anger, revealing them as the petty nuisances they are, while lifting us onto a higher plane.

Praise works because God made us in such a way that it will work. Does that sound like a circular riddle? Some of this may sound like pure psychology—power of positive thinking and all that. And that is exactly what it is. God is the one who created us with all our psychological traits. He made us the way we are long before the science of psychology was born. He is the Master Psychologist. He created us in such a way that when we praise, we are lifted above our troubles into a higher realm.

I do not like to think of praise as a gimmick to be used. I think of it rather as something which we are to obey. If we obey—sacrifice our self-pity, fear, anger, etc., on the altar of obedience—we will receive the psychological benefits which God instilled in us when we were created. "Be thankful, whatever the circumstances may be. For this is the will of God for you in Christ Jesus" (I Thess. 5:18).

Praise, whether of God, or just as a positive attitude, does have concrete results upon us. We are such complex people; we have so little conception of the vast mechanisms of our brains. But when we discover something that works, whether or not we understand it, we should take advantage of it.

I used to be puzzled by the fact that there were people who had no basis for a relationship with God. They never read the Bible, never went to church, knew nothing about Jesus as their Savior, and yet they seemed so happy. Then I knew others who read the scriptures daily, went to church consistently, and at one point in time had accepted Christ, but were always gloomy. How could this be?

Then I began to realize the secret. There are those who don't know God, but who have by nature or by choice decided to follow the way of love. Either they are naturally loving people or they have consciously made the decision to become loving persons. And in this love, they are linked to the positive energy which emanates from God. God is love, we are told by the apostle John. So that when we love, even when we have no belief in him, we are hooked up to his power.

But when we don't love, even though we have belief, we are not currently (excuse the pun) linked to his power. We are not walking in the Light. Neither of these analogies has anything to do with our salvation—that comes by belief. But this explains why some people who have no belief at all sometimes seem happier than those who do have knowledge of the Savior.

Praise is one way to love—whether we are loving God, or our fellow human beings. We should consciously praise God as part of our regular prayer time each day. But in addition to that, we should constantly thank him all day long for specific things which happen to us.

How do we praise God? What words do we use? In addition to thanking him, we should tell him that we love him and go over a list of his attributes. The Old Testament and the Psalms are good resources for the characteristics of God.

Juan Carlos Ortiz, an Assembly of God minister from Buenos Aires, has written a tremendous little book entitled *Disciple*. Regarding praise, he says: "What is praise? It is more than just using the word praise. If I am in a meeting where someone sings well, and I go to him afterward and say, 'Oh, I praise you, I praise you, I praise you,' that's not praise. I have to praise him *for* something. I should say, 'Listen, as you began to sing, my heart really responded to your message. I looked at the faces of the other people, and we were all caught up with your song.' "

He goes on to say that exclamations such as "Praise the Lord," "Allelulia," and "Glory to God" are all right, but not if they are only empty, meaningless phrases. We should praise the Lord *for* something. He says we bring all these praise "presents" to the altar, and yet when the Lord opens them, there is nothing inside. Our praise should have something inside. We should think of specific things for which we are grateful and thank God for these.

But there is also another way to praise God, although it should never be substituted for the type just described. That is praying in the Spirit.

When the day of Pentecost came, there were many foreigners in Jerusalem for the Passover. After listing all the many countries represented, the passage in Acts 2:11 goes on to say, "We can all hear these men speaking of the glorious works of God in our native language." Praising—that is what they were doing on the day of Pentecost and that is what we are doing now when we speak in tongues.

Paul writes in I Corinthians 14:4 that a "speaker in a 'tongue' builds up his own soul." Evidently, when we praise God, we build up our own souls; whether it is in our language or in our unknown prayer language, the results are the same. This is why and how praise works. This is the reason lives are changed when praise becomes a natural part of one's life. But we needn't have received the gift of tongues in order to praise. David lived long before the gifts of the Holy Spirit were given, and he certainly knew how to praise.

A few weeks after I had become a Christian, an Episcopal priest recommended a women's Bible study group. It was held on Wednesday mornings in a pretty little white frame Baptist church. I entered the sanctuary, where I was welcomed, and after a few announcements, the minister started the songs. The music was joyous; the women sang as if they really meant the words and were thoroughly enjoying themselves.

Then the minister began a lesson from the book of Hebrews. Being a novice at reading the Bible, I turned to the Old Testament. Hebrews certainly sounded like an Old Testament book to me! The woman sitting next to me reached over and gently found the correct section for me.

After a thorough study into one chapter, the minister asked for prayer requests. Women all over the room were telling of answers to prayer and asking for specific needs. Then the praying began. But it was different from any praying I had ever heard—it wasn't all in English. In a low murmuring tone, voices all around me were praying in what sounded like foreign languages.

I panicked. I had never heard of such a thing; I didn't know what the Bible said about this strange phenomenon, and I certainly didn't want any part of it. I got up and practically ran out of the church—certain I would never again go back to anything like that!

But as I began asking questions and studying the New Testament, I came to realize that this "speaking in tongues" as it is called was a very natural and normal part of life in the early church. It was evidence of the supernatural power of God, because others heard their own language being spoken by men who had no way of learning it. What was its purpose? What is its purpose today?

There is more than one reason for speaking in tongues. When a person first experiences this, it is a wonderful manifestation of the reality of God. It is a verification of the supernatural, and we all need this at some point in our lives. Many Christians have an intellectual belief in Christ, but when doubt creeps in, when living the Christian life becomes dull and ordinary, we need some sign that faith in God isn't just another philosophy; we need to experience his supernatural power.

I do not want to get into the controversy over the baptism of the Holy Spirit. If theologians dispute this point, I am certainly not qualified to take one side over the other. All I am dealing with here is praise, whether it is in our native language or in an unknown prayer language.

Another purpose of the gift of tongues is prophecy. This is used in public worship, but not unless there is someone with the gift of interpretation present. We are told to pray for this gift of interpretation.

Some are given direct messages for their own benefit, after having prayed in their prayer language. They pray, and then remain silent and listen to the Lord. He often interprets for them what they have just said.

Another very important reason for this type of prayer is its use when you are too depressed to pray any other way. How often have you felt that you just didn't know how to pray? How often have you heard others say, "I couldn't even pray." But that is the beauty of this gift. Paul tells us in the book of Romans that the Spirit prays for us at these times. And this is so true. In fact, it seems that to the degree you are down, praying in the Spirit lifts you up.

In other words, when everything is rosy and you are walking in close fellowship with the Lord, the sky is blue and the birds are singing, it is easy to come before his presence with thanksgiving and praise, as well as requests. But when you are down, really down, and don't feel worthy even to come into God's presence—when you really don't feel like praying—that is when praying in the Spirit means the most. This is because it is not you who is praying; it is the Holy Spirit. And as the Holy Spirit begins to praise God, you are brought up, up, up out of that depression, until finally you are at the point of being able to praise him with your conscious mind—in your own language.

This is not a gift we merit; it is a gift we seek, ask for. The Lord is a gentleman; he will not impose anything upon us that we do not want. Each must decide for himself whether or not to seek it.

Contrary to rumors, it is not an emotional manifestation; it is completely controllable. One can speak in tongues whenever one wishes, and stop at will. One can pray with the mind only, and not verbalize at all. It is nothing to be afraid of; it is a marvelous affirmation of the supernatural power of God.

But as I said before, the gift of tongues is not a prerequisite to praising God. Those who pray in tongues are no more "spiritual" than those who don't. They do have access to an additional method of prayer which is meaningful and helpful. However, those who do speak in tongues often get lazy and let the Spirit do all their praising for them, not devoting equal time to praising in their own language. The important thing is to praise—however it is done.

An incident in the life of a friend shows how praise can become such a natural part of our lives that when disaster threatens, praise carries us through.

Jan Potter, whom I mentioned before as being in my writers' group, was in labor with her second child. She and her husband had recently read *Prison to Praise,* by Merlin Carothers, and had begun the practice of systematically praising God in every circumstance.

123

She was having a slow labor, when suddenly the baby decided to skip a few steps in the normal process. Jan was rushed to the delivery room and almost immediately, the baby was born. But something was wrong. The child was motionless, silent, chalky white.

"Flick it on the feet!" a voice demanded. The doctor did so, but to no avail. He carried the baby to a table nearby, and the room became a mass of confusion as four people hovered over the infant, giving her oxygen, cleaning the passageway to the lungs, doing everything they could to save the newborn.

Jan was awake and alert, aware of everything that was going on. She breathed a prayer, "Lord, please let the baby live; let her be all right." Then she realized that the Lord wanted her to trust him and to believe that in his infinite wisdom, he knew what he was doing. So she thanked Jesus for the baby, no matter what happened.

As she continued openly praising the Lord, he worked a miracle! In the midst of total chaos, Jan became completely saturated with a wonderful, perfect peace like nothing she had ever experienced. She wasn't filled with an inner assurance that the child would live. But she had connected with the positive power of praise; she had dispelled fear and doubt and evil from that room by the mysterious power of praise.

Then she heard the most precious sound in the world: the faint cry of her newborn baby girl. Five long minutes had elapsed since the birth, and the baby was alive!

Of course, now there was a reason to praise God. But Jan hadn't waited for the results. She had begun praising God in the midst of her trouble, before she knew the baby would live. And once again, the mysterious power of praise did its work.

Recently, I visited a tiny Episcopal church in Newport Beach, California, where we were vacationing. The beautiful stained-glass windows, and the rich mahogany of the altar and pews spoke of all the years of tradition behind this dignified and worshipful atmosphere.

The offering was near the end of the order of worship, and as the plates were brought forward and the words of the Doxology began, the people of the congregation stood, put their hymnbooks down, and lifted their arms high toward heaven as they sang "Praise God from whom all blessings flow. . . ."

Yes, renewal is beginning in the churches. Praise is returning. The prayer of praise is lifting us all into a higher realm.

Chapter XI

The Power to Heal

The woman was middle-aged, but looked far older. The lines etched on her face reflected the pain she had suffered for so long. She had sought relief for twelve years; for twelve years she had gone from one physician to another. Her money was gone; she had given up hope.

She was weak; twelve years of a steady hemmorrhage—it was a wonder she was still alive. There had been many infections; many months when she had lain in bed, unable to care for her family. But she was stubborn; she had refused to give in to her illness. Whenever she heard of a new remedy, whenever she was told of a physician, she had sought help. But always, the hemmorrhage returned.

Then, someone told her about this man from Nazareth. He was a Jew who claimed to be from Jehovah. It was said he had miraculous healing powers. Maybe he would be able to help her!

When her daughter came rushing in to tell her that Jesus was approaching, followed by a large crowd, she immediately went out.

As he approached, she caught a glimpse of his face. And she knew—knew as she had never known before—that here was someone who had power, a power no one else possessed.

She tried to get near him, to speak to him, to tell him what was wrong with her. But the crowd was so large; they were shoving each other, fighting to get near him. It seemed impossible to get close enough to speak to him.

"If only I can touch his clothes," she said to herself, "I will be all right."

Finally, she worked her way through the crowd until she was right behind him. She reached down and touched the very hem of his cloak. At that instant the hemmorrhage ceased! She felt it; she knew within herself that she was cured!

She stood up and as she did, she was startled to see that Jesus had stopped. He turned and searched the faces of those around him.

"Who touched my clothes?" he asked.

His disciples replied, "You can see this crowd jostling you. How can you ask, 'Who touched me?' "

Then the woman, frightened and shaking all over because she knew she was the one to whom this thing had happened, came and flung herself before him. But he said to her, "Daughter, it is your faith that has healed you. Go home in peace, and be free from your trouble" (Mark 5:25-34).

Wherever Jesus went, crowds followed. They came to hear his message, but they also brought their sick. And in each instance, he healed them.

Why—what was his motive? Were the miracles of healing meant as signs? Were they for the purpose of authenticating his claims to be the Son of God? If so, why did he so often admonish those he had healed to go away and not tell anyone?

From reading the accounts of the miracles of healing in the New Testament, I have come to the conclusion that Jesus healed for only one reason—he saw the people's need. Since it was in his power to heal, since he had more compassion than any of us can even imagine, and since he was and is the Author of love, he had no choice—he healed them.

It is interesting to use a concordance and look up every instance in which our Lord healed someone. Distinct characteristics become evident as one reads story after story of Jesus' ministry of healing.

One of the aspects which struck me was that, in all cases except one, he healed every person who was brought to him, or whom he noticed needed to be healed. He must have cured many more than are specifically mentioned, as evidenced by the following verses:

Indeed, he healed all who were ill. (Matt. 8:16)

When Jesus emerged from his retreat he saw a vast crowd and was very deeply moved and healed the sick among them. (Matt. 14:14)

. . . and brought all the diseased to him. They implored him to let them "touch just the edge of his cloak," and all those who did so were completely cured. (Matt. 14:35)

And great crowds came to him, bringing with them people who were lame, blind, crippled, dumb and many others. They simply laid them at his feet and he healed them. (Matt. 15:30)

Vast crowds followed him, and he healed them there. (Matt. 19:2)

Only once did Jesus single out one person for healing and leave without healing others. The text in John 5:2-9 says Jesus healed the impotent man at the pool of Bethesda, and then moved away because of the great crowd. He was criticized by the Pharisees for healing on the Sabbath, so this might have been the reason for his not remaining to heal everyone in this instance.

As soon as Jesus chose the twelve apostles, he sent them out with instructions to heal the sick. Soon after, he sent out seventy more disciples with the same orders. The early church considered healing an essential part of its ministry, and now again, in the past few years, the rise in the number of miracles of healing is causing us to change our ideas about this. But what happened in between? Why did so many years elapse without many healing miracles? The key seems to be with us—not with God. God is the same yesterday, today, and forever. But when there is a diminishing of faith, there are diminished miracles.

Jesus went to his hometown of Nazareth and found nothing but doubt and mockery. He did cure a few, but the throngs weren't there to meet him; the news of his power to heal didn't impress the hometown folk. Their lack of faith inhibited his work.

So it was in the middle centuries. It isn't that miracles didn't happen at all. But they were rare, rare because of lack of faith. Some say there are dispensations—certain times when God does certain things. They say healings were necessary in the early church as signs of faith, and are not needed today.

Not needed today! If they were ever needed, it is today. It is true we have more knowledge of medicine than ever before, but it is also true that there is increasing illness. As was mentioned in the chapter about God's will, our pollution of the environment has brought new and more devastating diseases. And now, more than ever, we are in need of signs from God.

Historically, there was a subtle shift in church thinking in the fourth and fifth centuries A.D. Before that time, healing was considered to be God's normal will. The shift in doctrine grew over the centuries to the point that now we are more prone to think of sickness, rather than healing, as God's will. This view is more pagan than Christian; the gods of primitive peoples were always vengeful and full of dire punishments.

In the early church there was a gradual growth of belief in the dichotomy of the body and the spirit. The body was evil; the spirit, good. The more one could subdue the body (illness being one way to conquer it), the more spiritual one would be. This belief evolved into the extreme asceticism of the monks in the medieval centuries, along with self-abuse and flagellations of the body.

All this is totally contrary to scriptural teaching. Christ always treated illness as an enemy, a manifestation of evil. He did not make a division between the body and the soul, as we do. He wanted to make the entire person whole. He healed the body, and in most instances, this act of healing transformed the spirit, also.

130

If it is God's will for us to suffer, why do we go to doctors? Why do we take medicine? Isn't this going against God's will—doesn't he want us to be sick? Of course I am being facetious, but if one thinks this through logically, it is the conclusion to which one must arrive.

The book *None of These Diseases,* by S. I. McMillen, M.D., traces the cause of so many of our illnesses to our self-destructive ways. He shows how many, if not most, of our illnesses are self-induced by bad diet or poor emotional habits—in short, disregarding the clear teaching of scripture. He quotes from Dr. William Sadler, a psychiatrist: "More than one half of the present afflictions of mankind could be prevented by the tremendous prophylactic power of actually living up to the personal and practical teachings of Christ."

Not only do we not live the way he would want, but we do not obey his admonitions to go forth and heal. Or if we do pray for healing, it is as a last resort, or half-heartedly, not expectantly, in faith.

In reading books by those in the healing ministry, I was impressed by the fact that none of them had a sudden revelation; none of them were visited by an angel in the night, who told them they were to begin a healing ministry. In each case, they either were healed themselves, or they saw someone healed, and became interested. Then they began timidly, with doubts, but nevertheless they started, one step at a time. They waited for an opportunity to pray for someone's healing, and then they simply did it.

As they began this new venture, they grew in confidence. Not everyone was healed—then or now. But many were. And as with anything else, they learned as they took these first small steps of faith.

Many have been turned off the ministry of healing by the specter of the fiery-eyed evangelist on television, shouting in a loud voice, and commanding the poor sick person to "Be healed!" But occasional abuse of the gift doesn't mean we should discount the entire ministry.

It is true that some seem to have a special gift of healing (I Cor. 12:9). But this doesn't mean the rest of us can't pray for healing. We are too timid; we seem to think we are exalting ourselves if we try to heal. But what we must remember is that *we* never heal—*God* is the one who heals. All we do is pray, and certainly we all can pray!

We need to keep in mind always that the healing power is God's love. This love must be transmitted from God, through us, to the person asking for healing. This is one reason the laying on of hands seems to be more effective than when there is no personal contact. The positive energy present in the person praying transmits the healing love of God. The "healer" is nothing more than a conduit, a passageway for the love to flow into the one being prayed for. Again and again in the Gospel accounts of Jesus' healing, there is mention of his touching the persons in some way.

When I began to think about why this would be so, I realized if I were going to lay hands on someone, it would first be necessary to be in their presence. Does this sound elementary? Think about it. How often have you actually prayed for someone's health *in that person's presence?* Don't we usually just pray for someone from a distance, as part of our regular prayer time? Actually going to where someone is, in order to administer a healing prayer, takes some effort; it takes enough caring to get up and go to them.

Is this what James meant when he wrote, "Faith without works is dead"? We have faith that God will heal, but we aren't concerned enough to be the carrier of that message to others.

Father Francis McNutt, a Roman Catholic priest active in the healing ministry, says this work must be carried out by all of us, not by just a few people like him and his team. He believes the most natural people to pray for someone who is ill are those who love him, those who are around that person all the time. Father McNutt comes into a town only once a year, or perhaps only once ever, and he cannot possibly reach everyone. What he is teaching in his meetings now, is that each of us is called to this ministry—we must all be obedient to the call of Jesus to go forth and heal the sick.

When we are close to a person, we know all or most of the circumstances surrounding his life. We may intuitively know some reason for his illness and/or we may suspect why he is not being healed.

If our prayers are offered in a atmosphere of trust and concern, there is much more chance of a successful understanding of the problem. Persons who conduct healing ministries in large groups cannot possibly reach all those who are in need. This is exactly why they are telling us that we must all learn to participate.

For example, resentment is said to be the root of many diseases, and the antidote for resentment is forgiveness. If you suspect someone is harboring resentment, and because of that has become ill, you can (through repeated visits and a gradual building of confidence) gently point this out to the person. Often, all that is needed is confession and repentance—those are healings acts in themselves.

Our human reluctance to pray for healing is typified by an incident in the life of a friend, Barbara Denison. Barbara had recently read several books about healing, and had attended one of Father McNutt's meetings when someone she knew personally was healed. She fervently believed in the ability of all believers to pray for healing, but until an accident occurred in her home, it was just an intellectual belief.

Her son, Tom, is a typically active thirteen-year-old who seems to be out of one cast and into another. On this particular day, he had caught his finger in the sprocket chain on his bicycle. There was a deep cut across the middle of his fingernail which was bleeding profusely. Barbara knew there was no use taking him to the emergency room since no sutures could be taken in the nail.

She washed his finger and wrapped it up, telling Tom to hold the bandage firmly so as to stop the bleeding. All this time, he had been complaining loudly—he was in excruciating pain.

Suddenly, Barbara realized she should pray for the healing of his finger. If she really believed in the power of prayer, this was the time to show it. But there was a problem; Barbara was a relatively new Christian, and she had never prayed with her son. If he were younger, it wouldn't have been so hard, but she was embarrassed to pray for his healing in front of him.

She left him with some ice to help the pain and went into the living room, pacing up and down nervously. Finally, she decided she must do it, and she went back into Tom's room.

"Tommy, would you want me to pray for your finger?" she asked timidly.

"Yes!" came the quick reply.

His easy answer so startled her, she had to go into the living room again and pray for God to help her. Then she went back to him and prayed that the pain would go away and that the finger would heal quickly. Relieved, she left him again.

Five minutes later, Tom sauntered into the kitchen, smiling. "Guess what, Mom? The pain is all gone!"

No one was more surprised than Barbara. The prayer for healing had worked! Not only was the pain gone, but the finger healed so rapidly in the next few days, they were amazed.

James 5:14-16 tells us: "If anyone is ill he should send for the church elders. They should pray over him, anointing him with oil in the Lord's name. Believing prayer will save the sick man; the Lord will restore him and any sins that he has committed will be forgiven." The next verse goes on, "You should get into the habit of admitting your sins to each other, and praying for each other, so that you may be healed."

The anointing with oil is a neglected aspect of prayer for healing. Of course, the oil itself has no curative powers, but again, in order to administer oil (symbolic of the Holy Spirit), one must be there. One must touch the sick person. Prayer at bedtime for a list of sick people isn't the same as actually sacrificing one's time, and sometimes one's sophistication, to go to someone and pray for his healing.

The oil may be of any type (olive oil is commonly used), and many testify to having more success when using oil. It is biblical, and therefore should not be discounted.

Father McNutt says he is learning that many diseases aren't healed by one prayer, but show gradual improvement over a period of time, with a series of prayers. These are called "soaking prayers." We pray for the afflicted one and then let him "soak" in our prayers, adding to the solution of prayer daily, or at least regularly. Think of it as being soaked in a bath of love.

An example of this steadfastness in prayer, as well as the power of praise, occurred in the life of Jeff Nick, son of Pat and Tom Nick of Phoenix.

In the fall of 1971, Jeff was sixteen, a strapping two hundred twenty-pound football player. He and his identical twin, John, were in their junior year of high school. When Jeff's appetite began to slack off, his mother didn't think too much of it and, in fact, even encouraged Jeff's twin to follow his example. It wasn't until the boys' grandmother came to visit and noticed a change in Jeff's appearance that it was decided to send him for a checkup.

The family doctor was worried when he viewed Jeff's X-rays, and referred them to a specialist. After examining Jeff and seeing the X-rays, the doctor didn't mince words. "Jeff has a malignancy; it is inoperable, and probably terminal."

Inoperable! Terminal! It couldn't be! Jeff hadn't even complained; this was just a routine checkup. The finality in the doctor's voice sunk like a dead weight in Pat's chest. But her husband immediately said, "Well, praise the Lord!"

Pat was as shocked as the doctor when Tom said those words, but she immediately realized that she, too, must praise him even in this situation.

The doctor added that he wanted to put Jeff into the hospital right away to do a biopsy; this would help them determine the nature of the malignancy.

The Nicks were a Christian family. They were well-grounded in the Bible and lived in a very close relationship with Christ, so when this crisis came, they were not without a means of sustaining themselves. That night after dinner, Tom said he would like to go for a drive by himself to think and pray, and Pat found time to go into the bedroom alone. There in the quiet, she simply told the Lord she needed him to be with them. And as she prayed, she received an assurance from him; God told her he was going to give her the privilege of going through this trial with him. Pat was filled with a sense of peace. When Tom came back, he was excited; he ran in to tell Pat the Lord had told him he would be with them; he had experienced the very same assurance!

In obedience to the admonition in the book of James, Tom called the elders of their church that very evening and Jeff was taken to the church for prayer. The elders laid hands on him, anointed him with oil, and prayed for his healing.

The next day Jeff entered the hospital, and the biopsy was done. The verdict was Hodgkin's disease, a lymphatic cancer. He was subsequently sent to a hematologist, who said there was total involvement of his lungs. Still further testing was needed to determine the extent of the disease, and Jeff underwent a lymphangiogram, as well as a liver biopsy and surgery to remove his spleen.

The night after surgery, the Nicks were told Jeff might have a hard time breathing, but when they left the hospital that evening, Jeff seemed to be doing quite well. Pat and Tom had gone to bed when the phone rang. Tom answered, and was given the grim report: Jeff's temperature had reached 106°; his breathing was so shallow he had been given artificial respiration. He was in intensive care and packed in ice. The doctor's voice dropped: "All I can say is that the situation is quite serious; there is no guarantee Jeff will make it through the night."

Pat and Tom sat up in bed and looked at each other. "You know," Pat said, "God is asking us to relinquish our son. If we go to the hospital, what can we do but pray, and we can pray right here. We can wring our hands and Jeff wouldn't know we were there, but God can meet Jeff there at that hospital bed. All we need to do is give up our right to Jeff and trust God to do what he will."

Then after a time of prayer together, they did an incredible thing—they both fell sound asleep! Pat still can't believe they did that—but it's true. They so completely trusted God to do what was best for Jeff that not only did they not rush to the hospital, but they were able to get a good night's rest. Jeff was much better the next morning, although still in serious condition.

During that week, the members of their church, Calvary Church of the Valley, had gathered around in support. One by one they came, always with their Bibles, and ministered to Jeff by reading the scriptures to him. One day while he was still in intensive care, Pat and a friend took turns reading out loud all day. Jeff seemed to be asleep, but they knew the comforting words of scripture can break through to the subconscious mind and work their healing power. Pat feels that was a turning point; Jeff did survive the ordeal of surgery.

None of the test results had been disclosed to the Nicks. The doctors were waiting until all the data were in before any prognosis was made. But a meeting was scheduled at their church on the evening the results were to be given. No matter what the tests revealed, praise was going to be given to the Father.

When Pat saw the doctor approaching that afternoon, she noticed that for the first time, he was smiling. "Mrs. Nick," he began, "when we did the liver biopsy and removed the spleen, we felt sure there was total liver involvement. The cancer is present in the abdomen, but it isn't in the bone marrow, the liver, spleen, or in the blood!"

This was a small victory, but it was the first encouragement they received. The praise meeting was held on schedule.

It had only been two weeks since the diagnosis was first made, but now it seemed all the symptoms of the disease began to manifest themselves. Jeff's glands swelled and he suffered terrible itching. Hard crusts of skin formed on the bottoms of his feet. He started to lose weight; he was beginning what would end as a seventy-pound weight loss.

The next step was radiation therapy. The Nicks had prayed for guidance about this and felt it was the route they were to take.

Their first encounter with the radiation therapist was pretty discouraging. He explained to them, "I have never taken a patient in this advanced stage of the disease. Jeff's involvement is so extensive it is hopeless. The radiation may kill him," he went on. "I don't give him any more than a fifty-fifty chance to survive the treatment." Then he recommended a palliative dose, just enough to make Jeff feel better, so he could live a little longer.

However, the hematologist intervened. He called the radiation therapist and said: "Why don't we just go ahead and go all out in this case? The Nicks have such optimism; they want their son to live, not just to prolong his life for a while. Why don't we take a chance?" To this day, the Nicks feel God spoke through that servant of his to use this method of healing.

And so Jeff began the terrible ordeal of radiation therapy. As they took him down to the cold sterility of the radiology clinic every day, Pat and Tom began to realize they needed to do something to combat the terrible negativism which prevailed there.

Thus began what came to be called the Nicks' Open House. They put a sign on their door at home which read, "Enter into his gate with thanksgiving and into his courts with praise." Their house was literally open for people to come and go between the hours of 9:30 and 12:00 every day. People from the church would gather in groups of two or more during these hours and pray for Jeff to withstand the negative feelings of the hospital atmosphere, as well as the pain from the therapy. If he had a specific complaint, a note would be left asking them to pray especially for that, and it would be done.

About that time, Kenneth Hagin, an evangelist with a healing ministry, came to Phoenix. Pat and Tom felt they should take Jeff to this meeting because, although his faith was growing, there seemed to be a terrible oppression which was further intensified by the treatments. Physically, he was getting worse.

When Jeff went forward to the altar for healing, Kenneth Hagin placed his hand on Jeff's head and, much to Jeff's surprise, rebuked Satan. No one had had the discernment before to realize that this must be done.

Soon afterward, Roxanne Brant was in Phoenix for a series of healing meetings. A private interview was set up with her for Jeff, and in that hour, she spoke a harsh word of prophecy. She told Jeff that in ninety days, he would be either healed or dead. She said he was under one of the most terrible Satanic oppressions she had ever seen.

She looked at Jeff compassionately and said: "Jeff, you know, death isn't the end for Christians—I call it graduation day. You know you go to be with Jesus. You have eternal life because you have accepted him as your Savior. But you are only sixteen; maybe he has something for you to do here, on this earth. It has to be your choice. Do you want to stand up and fight this thing—and it won't be easy—or do you want to go on and be home with the Lord?" She left it up to him.

It took Jeff three days to make his decision—he decided to live. Roxanne had told him that if he decided to fight against the forces of Satan, the first step was to be baptized in the Holy Spirit. Jeff was a Christian; he did believe, but he had not yet come into that experience. In obedience, Jeff went to his pastor and asked him to pray with him for the baptism of the Holy Spirit. The pastor prayed, and Jeff immediately began to speak in a prayer language unknown to him, a verification for him that he had received the baptism.

Roxanne also had told him to gather together ten or twelve Spirit-filled believers who would stand together in prayer for him for an entire year. She explained that after this critical ninety-day period, he would be healed, but he would need these people standing by him in prayer, in order to keep his healing. This was quite a commitment for those people to make; yet not one person hesitated.

The radiation therapy was over on April 6, and as they went into the doctor's office, he looked at Jeff and said, "Well, Jeff, I didn't expect to see you sitting here today. I'll tell you the truth; I never thought you would be alive through the treatments. But your mother told me at the very beginning she had faith, and I just want to tell you she had a lot more faith than I did." He went on to say he was unable to get all of the cancer with the radiation. He recommended an eight-week rest, after which they would begin chemotherapy.

By now they were halfway through the ninety-day period Roxanne had prophesied, and nothing was really changed. Physically, Jeff was still quite ill.

Then, almost at the end of the ninety days, another crisis occurred; Jeff developed a paralysis on the left side of the face. Tom rushed him to the hospital, where the doctors said this was an indication he was nearing the end.

The only way they could discern the extent of the neurological involvement was to do an angiogram, a very painful procedure. The Nicks felt this was not a decision they should make; they left it up to Jeff. When he was told, Jeff responded, "You know, I really feel they aren't going to find anything; I know this is just Satan's lie. But I want the doctor to see that nothing is there, so I'm going to go through with it, and I'm going to tell the doctors about my faith."

During the next few days, Jeff suffered through the angiogram, a brain scan, and more spinal taps. The result—absolutely nothing. There was no sign of a tumor anywhere, and Jeff's faith soared! The ninety-day period was over the day he was released from the neurological center, and it was as if the darkness suddenly lifted.

About the first of June, the eight-week period was over, and Jeff was to begin the chemotherapy. When the doctor examined him, he looked puzzled. "Well, apparently the symptoms are gone for now. I can't find any lumps or anything! Let's wait another thirty days."

A month later, Jeff returned. He had begun eating again and had gained fifteen pounds. But the doctor still couldn't find any symptoms. This time he said, "I can't give chemotherapy when there are no symptoms. Would you mind going back to the hospital for X-rays?"

Would they mind! That's exactly what they wanted to hear.

When the X-rays were read, absolutely no evidence of the disease could be found. The radiation therapist couldn't believe it.

In May of 1977, Jeff and his twin brother, John, graduated with high honors from Oral Roberts University. Later that month, one week apart, the twins were married. Jeff is twenty-two years old now and in excellent health.

An interesting adjunct to this story concerns John, the other twin. While he was at the university, approximately four years after Jeff's ordeal, John discovered a small lump in his neck (one of the early symptoms of Hodgkin's disease). A subsequent biopsy revealed he did have the disease.

Even though there was less extensive involvement than with his twin, John was subjected to the same treatment. After removal of his spleen, he went through months of radiation therapy.

A large group of students and faculty at the college prayed daily for John. Because his faith had been so strengthened by Jeff's healing, it was only a matter of a few months until all his symptoms quietly disappeared and he was able to go through the difficult months of radiation with virtually no side effects. In John's case, the enemy wasn't allowed to get a foothold before being bombarded with prayers of faith; hence the Lord's healing power had clear channels in which to work.

Yes, God does heal today, just as he did when on earth almost two thousand years ago. Jeff and John Nick know, just as the woman with the issue of blood knew, that in Jesus there is the power to heal.

But what if you have been praying a specific prayer, with faith, for years, and yet the prayer is not answered? What if you have prayed for someone's healing and they are not healed?

I believe you have lost nothing. At least you showed the person you cared enough to pray for him. Should that prayer be dropped—is this a sign it isn't the Lord's will to heal that person? Jeff Nick's slow triumph certainly illustrated the benefits of perseverance. We must keep on praying until or unless God shows us differently; sometimes he has something better in mind.

Jim and Lynn Saint are a young couple with a missionary background. In the fall of 1977 they were eagerly awaiting the arrival of their first child.

Nathaniel arrived two-and-a-half weeks late. However, eight hours after his birth, the Saints were told something was wrong with him. They learned he was born with Wernig-Hoffman's disease, a fairly rare genetic disease in which there is no muscle tone and the muscles gradually deteriorate. The doctor said the baby would have no more than six months to live.

For two months Nathaniel seemed to be doing well. During this period, a number of people, including Jim, had dreams or visions of Nathaniel running very fast. Of course, they interpreted these to mean that the Lord would heal him.

Then Nathaniel developed pneumonia, an expected complication. Soon his breathing became so labored they rushed him to the hospital. Jim and Lynn felt his life was now completely in God's hands, and they felt at peace.

That evening Lynn began to pray. With her eyes closed, but fully awake, she visualized Jesus walking down the corridor of the hospital. She thought, "Good, now he's going to heal Nathaniel." She asked Jesus to first bless the other two babies in the room, which he did by placing his hands on them tenderly. Then he walked over to the foot of Nathaniel's bed, picked him up, and held him in his arms. The room was bathed in a brilliant light. Lynn looked at the scene and suddenly realized that Nathaniel's body was still on the bed, but his spirit was in Jesus' arms!

She opened her eyes and looked at the clock. It was 11:45. At midnight, the doctor called to say Nathaniel was dead. Lynn replied, "I already know; I just saw Jesus take him."

Yes, Jesus does hear prayer; he does have the power to heal. And in little Nathaniel's case, it was the ultimate healing.